D1062294

Reprints of Economic Classics

INCOME, EMPLOYMENT, AND THE PRICE LEVEL

INCOME, EMPLOYMENT, AND THE PRICE LEVEL

NOTES ON LECTURES GIVEN AT THE UNIVERSITY OF CHICAGO
AUTUMN 1948 AND 1949

By
JACOB MARSCHAK
The University of Chicago
and
Cowles Commission for Research in Economics

Edited and with a Preface by
DAVID I. FAND
and
HARRY MARKOWITZ

REPRINTS OF ECONOMIC CLASSICS

AUGUSTUS M. KELLEY • PUBLISHER
NEW YORK • 1965

LIBRARY OF CONGRESS CATALOGUE CARD NUMBER
65-25861

PRINTED IN THE UNITED STATES OF AMERICA
by SENTRY PRESS, NEW YORK, N. Y. 10019

PREFACE

The past two decades have witnessed great activity in Economic Theory. Mathematical Economics, Keynesian Economics, Econometrics have all grown up in this period. Significantly these branches of economic science seem to be well suited for dealing with Policy questions in the Economic Sphere. This particular development is hardly surprising, for the great disturbances of the first world war and the structural changes brought about by the great depression have changed the scene enough so that the State's relation to the economic mechanism now is more than one of providing and enforcing the rules. In this changed and changing environment the economist has been expected to play a role different in many respects from his role before the first world war. From being an observer and, perhaps, interpreter he has evolved into an actor and participant. The development of macroeconomics and the growth of the other branches of economic theory we have just mentioned can in large measure be accounted for by the change in the role played by the economist. One may or may not approve of the changed role of the economist. An evaluation of these new branches of economic theory must base itself, however, on considerations more substantial than either the uses, perhaps premature, to which these branches of economics have been put or the fact unpleasant to some, that the economist now occupies a different position.

In his lectures, Professor Marschak has set himself the task of incorporating these new developments in Monetary Theory and presenting them in a logical, precise and rigorous manner. As a necessary part of this task he has attempted to reveal the precise nature of the new analytical equipment, the problems it is intended to illuminate, the gaps in the older theory it fills and, in a general way, to synthesize the old and the new, distilling out the best in both. That this was a task that should have been done goes without saying, especially when it is remembered that a whole new generation of economists has appeared since the inception of these developments. It is to be hoped that with the publication of these lectures a serious gap in the literature of economic theory has been filled.

The plan of these lectures is relatively straightforward. In them Marschak analyzes the determination of major economic variables such as national income, output, price level, and employment. These economic variables are shown to depend on other variables more or less external to economic processes; e.g., political decisions, psychological propensities, technology. Thus, given the latter "external" or *exogenous* conditions, one can state a system of economic "behavior relations." Each such relation describes the behavior of a certain social group in a certain market. The simultaneous interplay of these relations determines the levels of the economic variables (the *endogenous* or "internal" variables of the economic system).

The behavior relations studied are of *macro-economic* nature: they are relationships like that between national income and aggregate demand of consumers; or like that between "the interest rate" and aggregate investment by business.

The macro-economic relations in turn can themselves be derived from more basic relations; i.e., the behavior patterns of single firms and households. The latter are called *micro-economic* relations. *Aggregation* is the process of inferring from micro- to macro-economics. Marschak shows how alternative assumptions concerning macro-economic relationships lead to different relations between endogenous and exogenous variables.

In particular, the following sets of alternative assumptions have been discussed. The labor market can be regulated by unions, or it can be free. The workers and/or employers, in determining the supply of, or demand for, labor can be affected by money wage rates, or by real wage rates. The consumers and businessmen can determine their purchases of goods in terms of physical quantities, or in terms of money expenditures. The demand for cash may be more or less elastic with respect to the interest rate. Stocks of cash may or may not affect the buyers of goods. And so on.

Each set of assumptions forms a different model, and yields different implications. For example, under one set of assumptions, the conclusion is obtained that no monetary or fiscal policy can affect the level of output; while under another set of assumptions, one derives the possibility of affecting employment by such means. If one believes certain assumptions about the behavior of workers and employers, it follows that "involuntary unemployment" in the following sense may ensue: no wage reduction conceded by workers can lead to more jobs. Under other assumptions, involuntary employment in quite a different sense may ensue: the demand for labor can fall short of its supply. The need for the empirical measurement of economic relations becomes obvious.

Finally, to sum up, the reader will find here illuminating remarks on such diverse topics as behavior equation, equilibrium conditions, aggregation, economic models, etc. Last but not least he will gain a real appreciation of the power of mathematical methods in clarifying economic theories, in enabling one to examine carefully the basic assumptions of these theories, in enabling one to gain mastery over them.

For these reasons, as students of Professor Marschak, we felt that it would be a real service to make these lectures available to a wider public. We must stress, however, that the material is provisional. It has not undergone systematic correction or revision b the author. The latter must wait until some much later date, at which time it is hoped to incorporate the contents of these lecture into a more complete work.

David I. Fand
Harry Markowitz

ACKNOWLEDGEMENTS

Grateful acknowledgement is made to Mr. Norman Breckner for the care taken in preparing the manuscript and to Mr. George Furiya for the skill and perseverance shown in Vari-Typing the manuscript for reproduction by photo-offset.

TABLE OF CONTENTS

LECTURES Page

PROBLEMS *"(Solutions will be made available separately.)"*

Lecture I: THE LOGIC OF ECONOMIC POLICY

This is a course in macro-economics. It deals with aggregates such as the total expenditure on consumption goods, total income, total demand for labor, etc. rather than with the demand or supply of single firms or families for single commodities. The relations between aggregates have to be consistent, to be sure, with our knowledge of the behavior of single firms or households with regard to single goods.

Macro-economic analysis helps to judge the effect of policies upon some particularly important aggregates. During the course considerable attention will be devoted, for example, to the controversy about the effect of fiscal, monetary and wage policies upon real national income. Roughly speaking, the "Keynesian" approach emphasizes the possibility of affecting real income by fiscal and monetary policies, under certain conditions, and tends to minimize the effect of money wage rates upon real income. The pre-Keynesian economics, on the other hand, largely neglected the effect of fiscal and monetary policy upon real income, and expected economic recovery from cuts in money wage rates. Crudely,

TABLE 1.I

	EFFECT UPON REAL INCOME	
	KEYNES	PRE-KEYNES
of Government demand	+	0
of money quantity	+	0
of money wage-rate	0	−

Generally, policy consists in choosing a set of actions (A), that will give the best set of results (R), given a set of uncontrolled conditions (C). In symbols,

(1.1) $R = \phi(A, C)$,

where
(1.2)
$R \equiv$ set $\{r'(\text{income, say}), r''(\text{price-level}), r'''(\text{inequality of incomes}), \ldots\}$

$A \equiv$ set $\{a'(\text{fiscal policy}), a''(\text{money policy}), a''', \ldots\}$

$C \equiv$ set $\{c'(\text{tastes}), c''(\text{technology}), c'''(\text{resources}). \ldots\}$

A policy matrix:

TABLE 1.II

	C_1	C_2	C_3 . . . .
A_1	R_{11}	R_{12}	R_{13} . . . .
A_2	R_{21}	R_{22}	R_{23} . . . .
A_3	. . . .		

Suppose conditions are C_2. We choose the best result among R_{12},

$R_{22}, \ldots$; if the best is R_{12}, we choose A_1. This is the essence of any practical action. In a competitive market, for example, the prices and technology are given, (C), and the entrepreneur chooses the output (A) such as would give him the highest profit (R); more generally, R indicates the best combination of profit and power, or of profits of successive years, rather than a single profit-figure.

Table 1.I (or, say, its "Keynesian" column) gave a detailed aspect of the policy matrix: viz., the effect of single policies (certain elements of the whole set of policies) upon a single element of the results, viz., the real income. Denote real income by y, and the government demand by G. Then the expression $\partial y/\partial G$ measures the effect of a unit change of government demand upon real income. Mathematicians call this measure a partial derivative. Economists use the term "marginal effect" or, in certain cases, "multiplier". We can study the effect of changing policies as well as the effect of changing customs. Remembering the notations (1.2) we have (as a general form of Table 1.I):

TABLE 1.III

	r'	r''	r'''
a'	$\frac{\partial r'}{\partial a'}$	$\frac{\partial r''}{\partial a'}$	. . . .
a''	$\frac{\partial r'}{\partial a''}$	$\frac{\partial r''}{\partial a''}$	. . . .
.	.	.	. . . .
c'	.	.	. .
c''	.	.	. .

The practical need is to know the elements in each cell, or at least to know whether they are zero, positive, or negative. If economic history had supplied us with a large number and variety of policies and conditions, or if we could experiment, we might use statistical estimation without further theorizing. Thus the effect of (controlled) fertilizing and (uncontrolled) weather upon the growth of plant is estimated from observations directly (method of multiple regression):

TABLE 1.IV

POLICIES AND CONDITIONS: \ RESULTS:	YIELD PER ACRE (y)
Amount of nitrogen (N)	$\partial y/\partial N$
Humidity (H)	$\partial y/\partial H$

Unfortunately, economic history gives only a small amount and variety of observations. We need additional information. This is drawn from scattered observations on the behavior of individuals, and is added to the more systematic data on economic aggregates. The name of economic theory is usually given to knowledge derived from information on individual behavior. In this sense, economic theory is needed to supplement aggregative data in order to estimate the effects of policies.

"(See also Supplementary Lecture I, pp. 69-70.)"

Lecture 2: INDIVIDUAL BEHAVIOR AND ECONOMIC POLICIES

A series of examples will illustrate how theories on the behavior of individuals can supplement aggregative data in deriving the effect of given policies and conditions upon economic aggregates.

It has been asserted that for every individual, (i), the ratio of his income (Y_i) to his cash (M_i) is a constant;

$Y_i / M_i = v_i$ = a constant;

$Y_i = M_i v_i$; therefore

(aggregate) $Y \equiv \Sigma Y_i = \Sigma M_i v_i$; but
(aggregate) $M = \Sigma M_i$ Now define the "average velocity of circulation", v:

$v \equiv \Sigma M_i v_i / \Sigma M_i = \Sigma M_i v_i / M$;

Then $Y/M = v$

(2.1) $Y = Mv$.

We shall use Roman capital letters for quantities of dollars (as in M), or quantities of dollars per unit of time (as in Y), or per unit of commodity or service (as in the case of prices or wage rates).

v is the "average velocity of circulation," weighted by the individuals' cash holdings. This is the weighted average of the individual v_i's, each being weighted by the individual's cash holding. With v thus defined it is constant as long as each individual's share in total cash remains unchanged; or, more generally, as long as the cash share of individuals having the same cash holding habits (expressed by v_i and depending on the frequency of income receipts and rent-payments and on other institutional factors such as holidays) remains unchanged.

From the verifiable assumption that v is constant, the marginal effect of M on Y is easily derived. A dollar increase in M increases Y by v dollars.

$dY/dM = v$.

The influence of M upon real income--say, y--is a more important thing to know. The measure or direction of this influence cannot be derived from (2.1) which does not involve real income. There is a definitional relation between real income, y, "price level", P, and money income, Y:

(2.2) $P = Y/y$.

This adds to our theory one equation but *two* unknowns. We shall need one more equation if we want to explain how y (and P) is determined by M.

Until further notice, we shall make a simplifying assumption that the prices of all products that constitute national output always change in the same proportion. That is, we are not interested in changes of relative prices between the products, and neglect such changes, thereby incurring, of course, a possibly sizable error. The assumption permits us to treat the whole output (real income) as a single commodity, measured in physical units, viz., in "dollar units of a basis-year."

A theory consisting of the two relations, (2.1) and (2.2), permits us to find, in terms of the knowns M and v, a single value of Y but not a single pair (P,y). We have, instead, a *relation* between (or "*restriction upon*") P and y, viz.,-- from (2.1) and (2.2)--

(2.3) $Py = Mv$,

known as the equation of exchange: see Graph 2:I.

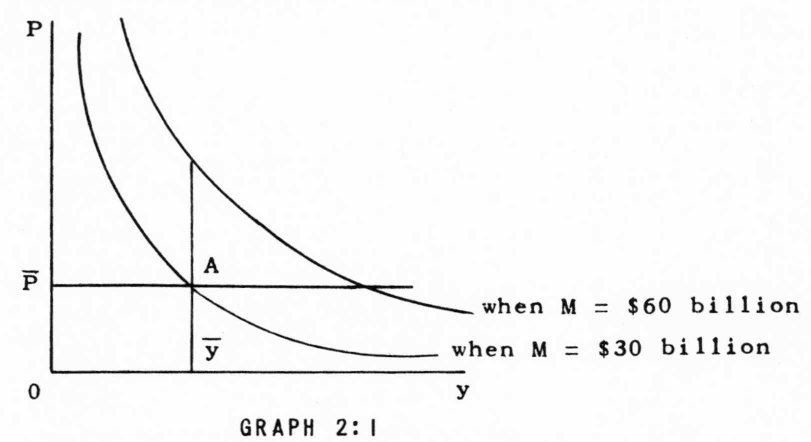

GRAPH 2:I

RELATION BETWEEN P AND y, AT CONSTANT v AND VARYING M

Each curve (it may be called "demand curve for all goods") is a "constant outlay curve" (= "demand curve of unit elasticity" = a rectangular hyperbola). As long as M and v are constant, P and y are connected by the relation which the curve represents: the area $\overline{P}A\overline{y}O$ is the same for all values $\overline{P}$, $\overline{y}$ of P, y. If either M or v rises, the curve "shifts upward."

The particular value which P and y take depends on M, v, *and* further conditions. A few examples of such an additional condition can be given:

(a). PRICE CONTROL. The government fixes P, that is, we have the relations:

(2.3) $Py = Mv$; (2.4a) $P = \overline{P}$

Real income, y, must then be

$y = Mv/\overline{P}$ (On Graph 2:I, see intersection of curve with horizontal line.)

(b). OUTPUT CONTROL. y is fixed.

(2.3) $Py = Mv$; (2.4b) $y = \overline{y}$.

Price must then settle at

$P = Mv/\overline{y}$. (On Graph 2:I, see intersection of curve with vertical line).

(c). LABOR THEORY OF VALUE. *(Example suggested by Mr. Weil, a member of the class.)*

(2.3) $Py = Mv$; (2.4c) $P = cW$; (2.4c') $W = \overline{W}$,

where $\overline{W}$ is the level at which government or unions fix the money wage rate W; and c is a constant. On Graph 2:I this case appears as a variant of case (a), with the $\overline{P}$-line shifting upward as $\overline{W}$ rises.

(d). A "*supply curve for all goods*," based on the idea that marginal product declines as output rises, and that real wage rate (W/P) offered by employers equals marginal product. (This superficial statement will be explored later more critically.)

(2.3) $Py = Mv$; (2.4d) $y = \sigma(P/W)$; (2.4d') $W = \overline{W}$,

where σ is an increasing function of P/W, and W is again assumed fixed "politically" at $\overline{W}$. On Graph 2:II, the two falling curves are the same as on 2:I;

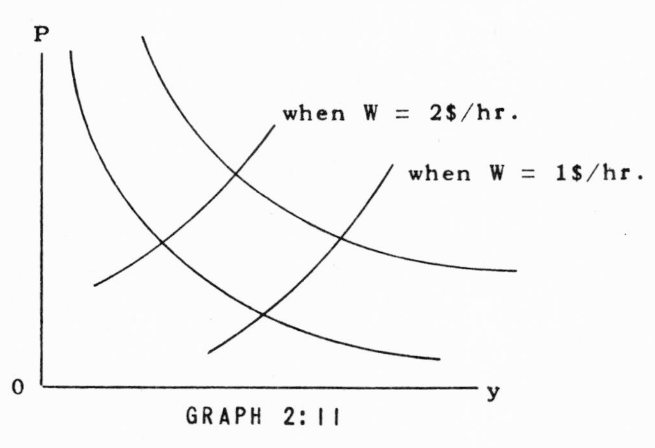

GRAPH 2:II

Introducing "supply curve for all goods" (depending on money-wage rate, W).

The two rising curves represent the supply relation between P and y at two different levels of the money wage rate, W, assumed to be fixed arbitrarily from outside; the higher W, the less is produced at a given price.

From the graphs, the sign of the effect of policies could be estimated, if we could assume that it is *possible* to fix M, $\overline{W}$ (and, as the case may be, $\overline{P}$, $\overline{y}$) while maintaining v and c unchanged. As long as we cannot assert that it is possible, the above theories are very weak, indeed. They have served to illustrate the logic of the problem. The following summary completes this illustration:

TABLE 2.1

EFFECT OF RAISING	UPON	REAL INCOME				PRICE LEVEL			
		(a)	*(b)*	*(c)*	*(d)*	*(a)*	*(b)*	*(c)*	*(d)*
M		+	0	+	+	0	+	0	+
$\overline{W}$		0	0	−	−	0	0	+	+

It will be remembered that v was assumed constant throughout; thus, for example, any possibility that a change in the money wage rate W can affect v through the redistribution of incomes is ruled out (for example, all individuals have the same velocities of circulation regardless of their income). More intricate models might relax this assumption.

Under each of the above theories the two variables were determined as depending on certain givens: viz., the "politically fixed" M, $\overline{W}$, and possible $\overline{P}$, $\overline{y}$; and on psychologically, sociologically, or technologically given quantities or functions, v, c, and σ. For example, under theory *(d)* we can write

$$(2.5)\quad y = \phi(M, \overline{W}, v, \sigma).$$

We shall always use ϕ to mean "depends on the values of symbols contained between the parentheses, and on nothing else."

Each of the four theories was logically complete and consistent; each contained as many unknowns as independent relations; and a solution for each of the unknowns--such as (2.5) for y--can be found. A complete and consistent theory can still be false, i.e., it may contradict facts. E.g., suppose it is known that money-wage rates are not fixed arbitrarily but are always related to, say, output. Then, in theories *(c)* and *(d)*, the equation $W = \overline{W}$ becomes false. If this equation is simply dropped, we obtain an incomplete theory. We have, rather, to search for some replacement for the dropped relation $W = \overline{W}$.

Lecture 3: DEMAND FOR GOODS (CONSUMPTION AND INVESTMENT EXPENDITURES)

In the theories of Lecture 2, the equation of exchange was derived from observed behavior of individuals, viz., from the habit or necessity of holding cash equal to the income of $1/v_i$ years, v_i being a constant characteristic of the individual i.

It followed that the aggregate M depends on the aggregate Y. The conclusion that Y can be manipulated by arbitrarily changing M required a logical jump: Y and y were interpreted as the demand for goods, in dollars or physical units respectively; and demand had to equate supply determined by certain additional factors (e.g., fixed output, technology, fixed wage-rate, etc.). But, it may be questioned whether income and demand (both being measured either in dollars or in physical units) are really the same thing.

The Keynesian analysis distinguishes demand for consumers' goods (C dollars, or c physical units, per year) and demand for investment goods (I dollars or i physical units, per year). Neglect provisionally the government as a buyer and tax collector. Unlike the equation of exchange, the following equations are supposed to be derived from observations on decisions to *demand goods* not from observations on decisions to *hold cash:*

(3.1) $C = \alpha(Y)$ (3.2) $I = \bar{I}$,

where $\alpha(\ )$ is a function depending on the distribution of income and of consumption habits, and where $\bar{I}$ is a constant.

(3.1) might be completed to include the effect of available cash upon the decision to consume:

(3.1a) $C = \alpha(Y, M)$;

but we postpone this refinement of the consumers' demand equation. We also postpone the discussion whether it is permissible to have a system without an equation of exchange or some other equation expressing the decision to hold cash. (3.1a) *is not* such an equation, but (2.1) is.

The symbol $\bar{I}$ in (3.2) expresses the investment level decided upon by firms and allegedly *independent of other economic variables.* Verbally, (3.2) is equivalent to the statement:

"I is exogenous (predetermined, autonomous)."

Again, various refinements of (3.2) will be discussed later.

A theory alternative to (3.1), (3.2) is

$$(3.1^*)\ c = \alpha^*(y)\ ;\ (3.2^*)\ i = \bar{i}\ ,$$

describing all decisions and the decision factors in physical rather than money terms. This important difference was overlooked in the discussions during depression, when prices were rather stable. In the present lecture, only the theories (3.1), (3.2) will be used. These two equations have three unknowns: C, Y, I. The missing equation is

$$(3.3)\ C + I = Y;$$

on the left hand we have total demand (in dollars); on the right hand we have money income, i.e., the sum of incomes: wages, interest, rents, profits paid out to factors (including profit-receivers) producing the output; this sum is identical with net output (*net:* we omit double counting of raw materials, and of wear and tear), or supply, in dollars per year. (3.3) says that total supply equals total demand, both in dollars per year. (3.3) can be thought of as expressing the fact that if demand exceeds supply (both in dollars per year) then either physical output or price level or both are raised by the businessmen very quickly until the excess demand vanishes. Thus, (3.3) is an "equilibrium condition": a departure from it is possible but must be short-lived. Thus demand and income are *not* the same thing; they merely *tend* to be equal. *(See first paragraph of this lecture).* But supply and income are the same thing.

The difference Y − (C + I) consists of produced but not demanded goods: the "undesired inventories" (the desired inventories are part of I). In equilibrium they vanish:

$$Y - (C + I) = 0$$

$$(3.3a)\ Y - C = I\ .$$

Y − C is called "savings"; hence, in equilibrium "savings equal investment". That is, a difference between savings and investment can be only short-lived and is therefore neglected, pending a more exact restatement.

The system (3.1), (3.2), (3.3) would explain the determination of Y as a function of the two givens: viz., of the fixed investment level $\bar{I}$, and of the function α;

$$(3.4)\ Y = \phi(I;\alpha),\ \text{say.}$$

For an arithmetic example, assume α linear. Measuring Y, C, I in $ billions a year, suppose

$$(3.1.A)\ C = 0.8Y + 5$$
$$(3.2.A)\ I = 35$$
$$(3.3.A)\ C + I = Y$$

By (3.3) and (3.2.A), C = Y − 35; Y − 35 = 0.8Y + 5; hence

$$(3.4A)\ Y = \frac{40}{1 - 0.8} = 200,\ \text{a special case of (3.4).}$$

For more useful (because more general) results, we need algebra:

(3.1.B) $C = \alpha_1 Y + \alpha_0$, say;
(3.2.B) $I = \bar{I}$
(3.3.B) $C + I = Y$

Solving as before:

$$(3.4.B)\ Y = \frac{\bar{I}}{1 - \alpha_1} + \frac{\alpha_0}{1 - \alpha_1},$$

a special case of (3.4) (α_0, α_1 are the two parameters of a linear function α and describe it completely). (3.4.B) implies that a rise in intended investment by 1 unit results in a rise of income by

$$\frac{1}{1 - \alpha_1} \text{ units.}$$

The expression $1/(1-\alpha_1)$ is thus equal to the derivative of Y with respect to $\bar{I}$, $\partial Y/\partial \bar{I}$, it being understood that the other givens (α_1, α_0) are not affected by the change in $\bar{I}$. This expression is called "the investment multiplier."

Lecture 4: EFFECT OF (EXOGENOUS) INVESTMENT UPON NATIONAL INCOME: A STATIC MODEL

Geometrical proof **that $m = 1/(1 - \alpha_1)$, where**

$m = \partial Y/\partial \bar{I}$ = "investment multiplier", and where

$\alpha_1 = d\alpha(Y)/dY$ = "marginal propensity to consume". (The function $\alpha(Y)$ is the "consumption function".)*

Consumption and *Total Demand Curves are linear.*

The slopes of angles ROY and SQT are, respectively, 1 and α_1.

When investment increases by $\overline{RS} = 1$, income increases by $\overline{QT} = \overline{RT} = m = 1/(1 - \alpha_1)$.

Proof: $m = \overline{QT} = \overline{RS} + \overline{ST} = 1 + m\alpha_1$.

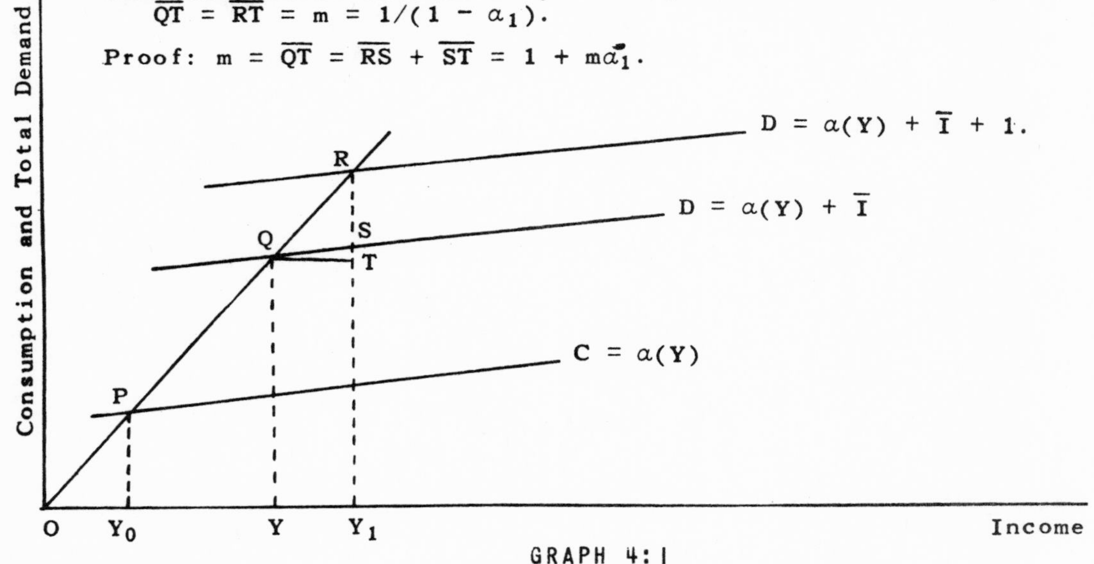

GRAPH 4:I

Suppose first that the consumption function, $C = \alpha(Y)$, is linear, with slope α_1. It is represented on Graph 4:I by the line through

---

* REMARKS ON NOTATION. In Lecture 1, the effects of changes in various policies or in non-controlled conditions upon an economic variable were written out as *partial* derivatives, e.g., $\partial Y/\partial G$. This emphasized that several policies or non-controlled conditions may change simultaneously, and that we have to take them up one by one. In the present lecture, investment level, I, is considered as the only condition that is susceptible to change. This justifies the use of the *total* derivative symbol, $dY/d\bar{I}$, for the investment multiplier. We concentrate attention upon the effects of changes in investment level and deliberately forget changes in other conditions. If changes in the function α (e.g., in the linear case, changes in the slope α_1, or the intercept α_0) were to be discussed, the partial symbol would be more helpful since quantities such as $\partial Y/\partial I$, $\partial Y/\partial \alpha_1$ would have to enter. Similarly, the marginal propensity to consume can be denoted as a total derivative $d\alpha(Y)/dY$--or, briefly, $d\alpha/dY$--since Y is here supposed to be the only argument of the consumption function. If consumers' demand depended, in addition, upon, say, money stock M, the more appropriate notation would be $\partial\alpha(Y, M)/\partial Y$, or briefly, $\partial\alpha/\partial Y$.

P; this renders the equation (3.1.B). If, as in equation (3.2), investment, I, is fixed at level $\overline{I}$, independently of income, total demand is represented by the line $D = \alpha(Y) + I$. If I is raised by $\overline{RS} = 1$ to $\overline{I} + 1$, total demand line becomes $D = \alpha(Y) + \overline{I} + 1$. The equilibrium condition, (3.3), is expressed by the line $\overline{OR}$, passing through the origin at a 45 degree angle to the Y-axis. When $I = \overline{I}$, equilibrium income $= \overline{OY} = \overline{QY}$; when $I = \overline{I} + 1$, equilibrium income $= \overline{OY} + \overline{QT}$. The multiplier $m = \overline{QT}/\overline{RS} = (\overline{RS} + \overline{ST})/\overline{RS} = 1 + \overline{ST} = 1 + m\alpha_1$. Hence, $m = 1/(1 - \alpha_1)$.

NOTE: when $\overline{I} = 0$, the equilibrium income $= \overline{OY_0}$; it was called "rock-bottom income". This is not the lowest possible income, since $\overline{I}$ may be negative when a nation lives on its capital, *i.e.*, depletes inventories and leaves equipment in disrepair.

The proof is valid even if the curve, C(Y), is *not* a straight line, provided the change in $\overline{I}$ is small, so that the relevant segment $\overline{QS}$ of the total demand curve can be approximated by a straight-line segment. That is, the marginal propensity to consume, *i.e.*, the slope of $\alpha_1 = dC(Y)/dY$, may change with the income, but its change within the considered range of income must be negligible.

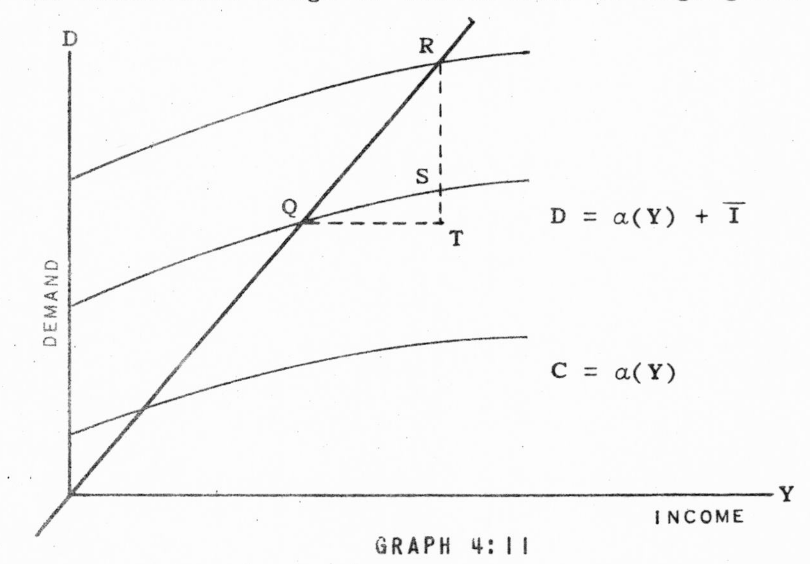

GRAPH 4:II

NON-LINEAR CONSUMPTION AND TOTAL DEMAND CURVES

On Graph 4:II, the consumption curve $\alpha(Y)$--and hence the total demand curve, $\alpha(Y) + I$--has its slope decreasing as Y increases: for example, the tangential straight line drawn to the D-curve at Q would be steeper than the tangential straight line drawn to the same curve at S. However, if $\overline{RS}$ (and consequently $\overline{QT}$) is small, the two tangential straight lines almost coincide with each other. (The arc $\widehat{QS}$ almost coincides with its cord).

NOTE: On Graph 4:II, the curved consumption line was restricted by the following conditions, deemed realistic:

(4.1) $0 < \alpha_1 < 1$;

(4.2) α_1 falls as Y rises (it is almost 1 for a very poor nation, and almost 0 for a very rich one);

(4.3) $\alpha(Y) > 0$.

These conditions were assumed valid for any positive Y. But this is too restrictive. For the theorem, $m = 1/(1 - \alpha_1)$, to be valid over some relevant range, it is sufficient to assume these conditions for that range only, and let the curve outside of that range behave in any plain or fancy way.

The system (3.1), (3.2), (3.3), if true, permits us to predict income, Y, for any given investment, I, provided the consumption function, $\alpha(Y)$, is known. If not all properties of $\alpha(Y)$ are known but only its derivative, α_1, for the relevant range of Y, it is still possible to predict the increment of Y--say, ΔY--resulting from a given small increase in investment, ΔI: vis., $\Delta Y = \Delta I/(1 - \alpha_1)$. Thus, if the initial income--say, Y_0--is known, it is possible to predict $Y = Y_0 + \Delta Y$, which will prevail as the result of a given change in investment, even though the knowledge of the consumption function is limited to that of the marginal propensity to consume, α_1.

Such predictions are of practical importance and were attempted during 1940-1945, especially when forecasts of the post-war situation were attempted. Suppose, for example, that

(4.4) $\alpha(Y) = .8Y + 5$.

Then (see Lecture 3), any pairs of values for Y, I are eligible, provided they satisfy the relation

(4.5) $Y = 5I + 25$. Examples of such value-pairs are: 10 and 75; 20 and 125; 30 and 175; 40 and 225, etc. The complete set of eligible pairs is given by all points on the straight line, (4.5). One can also obtain this complete set by shifting the total-demand-line on Graphs 4:I or 4:II by varying amounts and marking the equilibrium points. (In the case of Graph 4:II, a curved consumption line, the relation between Y and I also will be curvilinear.)

Instead of these quick and exhaustive methods, the method of piecemeal trial and error has been often applied in the literature of 1940-1945. A worker would try several pairs of values for Y, I to see whether they satisfy the condition, $Y = I + \alpha(Y)$. Each pair that withstood this test, together with figures for real income, employment, and unemployment that were derived from Y, constituted a "model"*. (To derive real income, an additional assumption was made regarding the price-level; employment was then derived from real income on the basis of some labor-productivity assumption. Un-

---

* In what follows, we shall occasionally use the term, "model", always identically with "system" or "theory". *E.g.*, (3.1), (3.2), (3.3) constitute a model. We shall not use any word to denote a particular set of figures that satisfies a model. Once the theory is formulated as a system of equations, the obtaining of eligible numerical values is trivial. Much of the literature on the subject lacks a clear formulation of the theory and the objective because the authors failed to write out the equations they had in mind.

employment was defined as the difference between employment and "labor force", or "maximum employment", based essentially on demographic data. A complication introduced by taxes will occupy us later.)

PROBLEM 3. Assume that the following variables (all measured in dollars per year) are predetermined: net private investment, government expenditure, tax receipts. Assume the following behavior relations:

(1) Consumption demand (dollars per year) = linear function of disposable national money income;
(2) Supply value (dollars per year) = demand value (dollars per year);

Write the following identities:

(3) Supply value = national money income;
(4) Demand value = consumption demand plus net private investment and government demand.

Express national money income as a function of predetermined variables only (write α_1 and α_0 for the slope and intercept of the linear "propensity to consume function ").

PROBLEM 4. In Problem 3, assume $\alpha_1 = 2/3$, $\alpha_0 =$ \$20 bill a year, private net investment = \$20 bill a year. Calculate the tax receipts and the government deficit, if the desired national money income is \$200 bill, and the government has committed itself to an expenditure of

a) \$20 bill or
b) \$40 bill or
c) \$60 bill

PROBLEM 5. Construct a diagram showing the results of Problem 4 and, in addition, the general relationship between government expenditures and tax receipts, if money income is to be \$200 bill and if the propensity to consume function and the private net investment are as in Problem 4. (Hint: express the tax receipts as a function of government expenditure, when all other magnitudes are given; insert from Problem 4 the numerical values of these givens; then plot the relationship of government expenditure to tax receipts.)

PROBLEM 6. Same as Problem 5, but the desired national money income is \$160 bill. Plot the result on the same diagram as Problem 5.

PROBLEM 7. Same as Problem 5, but assume α_1(marginal propensity to consume) = 4/5.

PROBLEM 8. Same as Problem 5, but assume private net investment = \$10 bill.

Lecture 5: AGGREGATION: AN EXAMPLE: INDIVIDUAL AND AGGREGATE DEMAND FOR CASH

Before proceeding further with the systematic development of macro-economic models, an interlude of three lecture periods served to discuss the relation of such models to the behavior of single individuals: the problem of "aggregation" or "transition from micro- to macro-economics." This was illustrated by two examples: (1) aggregate demand for cash; and (2) aggregate demand for consumers' goods --both as functions of aggregate income and, possibly, of other variables. Example (1) was the subject of an assignment given to students after Lecture 2; it requested them to check the statement that, in the U.S.A., the ration Y/M was constant over the period 1920-1948. (2) was assigned after Lecture 7, requesting them to estimate the relationship between C and Y under various alternative assumptions as to the changes in the frequency distribution of family incomes (changing cash family income by the same amount; or by the same percentage; or by transferring income from upper to lower brackets), using a sample of urban families with two or more persons, U.S., 1944 (*Statistical Abstract*, 1947, Table 307).

Inability to make experiments puts the economist at a disadvantage when compared with the natural scientist. This is partially redeemed by the economist's power of introspection into the plausible, or "understandable" (Max Weber) behavior of the smallest unit, the individual. It is plausible that the individual should determine his cash amount and his consumption expenditure as functions of his money income. Furthermore, it is possible to define general principles of consistent "rational behavior" (such as "maximizing utility") which would imply the existence of those functions: this is the subject of "micro-economics."

Consider the hypothesis

$$(5.1)\quad M_{\nu\tau} = k_\nu Y_{\nu\tau};\ \nu = 1, \ldots, n;\ \tau = 1, \ldots, t;$$

where ν identifies the individual and τ the point of time, so that the ratio $M_{\nu\tau}/Y_{\nu\tau} = k_\nu$ depends on the individual but not on time. k_ν is identical with $1/v$ of Lecture 2, where the aggregation of the hypothesis (5.1) over all individuals, using an appropriate definition of "average velocity of circulation" was discussed. However, (5.1) may be too narrow a case of the general relation

$$(5.2)\quad M_{\nu\tau} = \lambda_\nu(Y_{\nu\tau}),$$

where λ_ν is some function characteristic of the ν-th individual. To approximate (5.2) by a straight line for some relevant range of values--as on Graph 5:I--we may have to introduce an intercept l_ν, (positive or negative), in addition to the slope k_ν:

$$(5.3)\quad M_{\nu\tau} = k_\nu Y_{\nu\tau} + l_\nu,$$

even though the exact function itself is known to pass through the origin; *i.e.*, even if we should believe that people with zero-income demand zero-cash.

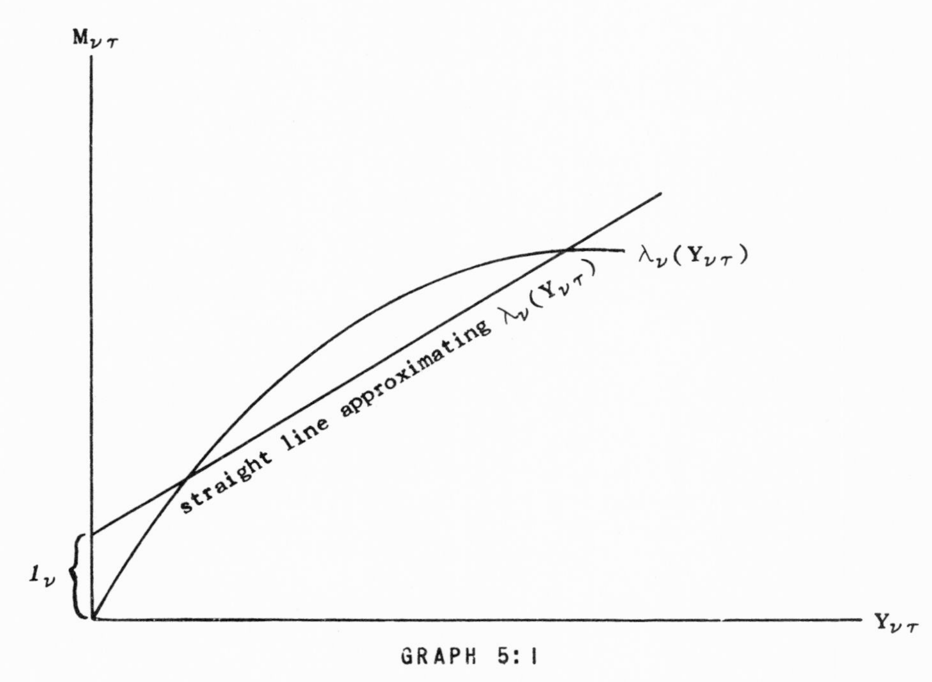

GRAPH 5:1

APPROXIMATING A NON-LINEAR RELATION BY A STRAIGHT LINE

Lecture 6: AGGREGATION: THE EXAMPLE (Continued)

Another direction in which the special hypothesis (5.1) may have to be generalized to explain the lack of constancy in the individual's "velocity of circulation" (or its reciprocal, k_ν), is to take into account further relevant variables, in addition to his income. For example, the interest rate--say, r_τ--may also affect his cash demand:

$$(6.1)\quad M_{\nu\tau} = \lambda_\nu(Y_{\nu\tau}, r_\tau),$$

the so-called "liquidity-preference function" for the individual ν. Or, using again a linear approximation,

$$(6.2)\quad M_{\nu\tau} = k_\nu Y_{\nu\tau} + m_\nu r_\tau + l_\nu,$$

where k_ν, m_ν, l_ν are characteristics of the ν-th individual. Graphically, (6.2) can be represented by a family of parallel straight lines: in the (Y,M)-plane, with k_ν as the slope and with r_τ responsible for "shifts"; or in the (r,M)-plane, with m_ν as the slope and with $Y_{\nu\tau}$ responsible for "shifts"; or in the (Y,r)-plane. Graph 6:I uses the first way of presentation; the changing intercept = $m_\nu v_\tau + l_\nu$.

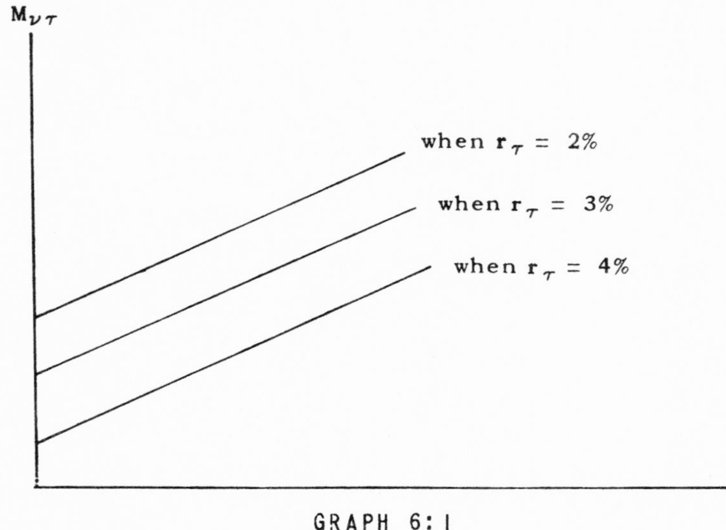

GRAPH 6:I

LIQUIDITY PREFERENCE EQUATION (6.2)

Summing up (6.2) over all individuals, $\nu = 1,\ldots,n$, we obtain

$$(6.3)\quad M_\tau = kY_\tau + mr_\tau + l;\ \tau = 1,\ldots,t,$$

provided the aggregates M, Y, and the "macro-economic" constants k, m, l are defined as follows (the summation sign Σ meaning here summation over individuals, not over time):

(6.4) $M_{\tau} = \Sigma M_{\nu\tau}$; $Y_{\tau} = \Sigma Y_{\nu\tau}$; $l = \Sigma l_{\nu}$; $m = \Sigma m_{\nu}$;

(6.5) $k = \Sigma k_{\nu} Y_{\nu\tau} / \Sigma Y_{\nu\tau}$ (*i.e.*, average of all k's, weighted by corresponding incomes).

Lecture 7: AGGREGATION OF RANDOM BEHAVIOR

We have seen that the lack of constancy of the ratio M/Y can be explained by the narrowness of the hypothesis (5.1) for each individual. His demand for cash may depend on income in ways other than simple proportionality; and it may depend on further variables, such as interest rate, price-level, number of children.

The number of variables (such as income, interest rate, etc.), each of which produces a sizeable--so-called "systematic"--effect upon M is limited. But in addition there is the erratic or "random" effect caused by simultaneous action of a host of further variables, each of which is responsible for a very small effect only. This is why the same individual may, at two points of time ($\tau = 1$, and $\tau = 2$) demand different cash even though his income, the interest rate, etc., are the same. This statistical ("stochastic," "random") nature of his behavior may be approximated by the following hypothesis:

$$(7.1)\quad M_{\nu\tau} = k_\nu Y_{\nu\tau} + m_\nu r_\tau + l_\nu + u_{\nu\tau};\ \nu = 1,\ldots,n;\ \tau = 1,\ldots,t,$$

where $u_{\nu\tau}$ is a "random deviation." (7.1) without the random term is defined to be the long-run average of the money demand of the νth individual. The $u_{\nu\tau}$ expresses random deviations from this average. It follows from this definition that the long-run average of $u_{\nu\tau}$ is zero. It is further assumed that while the individual's behavior thus fluctuates from day to day, these fluctuations have certain constant features: $u_{\nu\tau}$ takes certain values with certain probabilities. The long-run average of $u_{\nu\tau}$ (the statisticians' "expectation," or "expected value") is zero and $u_{\nu\tau}$ may, for example, have the following probability distribution:

$$(7.2)\quad \begin{cases} \qquad\qquad\qquad u_{\nu\tau} = \ -1;\quad 0;\quad +1 \\ \text{with probabilities: } 0.2;\ 0.6;\ 0.2 \end{cases}$$

Sometimes it may be possible to characterize the probability of distribution of $u_{\nu\tau}$ by a single number, e.g., the standard deviation, a measure of "fickleness" of the individual in his cash-holding behavior. Such a constant (or, if necessary, two or more such "statistical parameters"), together with the coefficients k_ν, m_ν, l_ν would give a full picture of the individual's cash-holding behavior, i.e., of the way his demand for cash responds to changes in his income, in the interest rate, etc. It enables us to make predictions, i.e., to tell the probability with which his cash-demand will fall into a given interval.

Suppose a society consists of a very large number of individuals. Suppose that each man $\nu (\nu = 1,\ldots n)$ is characterized by the same probability distribution (7.2) and fluctuates in his behavior, independently of other members of the society. Then, by the same reasoning as before, the average of all deviations occurring at the same time, say $u = (u_{1,\tau} + u_{2,\tau} + \ldots + u_{n,\tau})/n$ will tend to be zero: the larger n, the closer will u_τ approach zero. The same applies even if the individuals have different probability distributions (e.g., different standard deviations) of their behavior, provided that each fluctuates in his behavior independently of his neighbor. We would then have, for very large aggregates of men, exact functions such as (6.3), with no random term attached; while for small aggregates--e.g., the aggregate of the half-dozen or so automobile producers, even if considered mutually independent in their decisions--we would have sizeable random fluctuations from one time point to the next, and would have to write:

$$(7.3)\quad M_\tau = kY_\tau + mr_\tau + l + u_\tau,\ \tau = 1, \ldots, t,$$

where the values of u_τ for various points of time would be independent and would, in the long, average out into zero. But at every single point of time, the average deviation u_τ would, in general, be positive or negative, rarely zero. Only if the aggregate is large (i.e., n is large) would u_τ at each time τ be negligible, under our assumption of men making their decisions independently.

Suppose, however, that men do not make their decisions independently but are "keeping up with the Joneses". Then the average u_τ will be sizeable even though the society may be large. For example, if a fit of hoarding behavior affecting Mr. Jones is, more likely than not, accompanied by similar behavior of Mr. Smith, the positive deviation of Jones will not be offset by a negative deviation of Smith. Thus the deviation u_τ of the aggregate demand for cash from some exact function of aggregate income, interest rate, etc., will be larger, the larger the degree of dependence between the fluctuations in the behavior of individuals. (As an extreme example, consider the case when all individual deviations are "perfectly correlated", e.g., retain constant proportions to each other!)*

Macro-economic relations are usually "stochastic". They look like (7.3) rather than (6.3); even after all relevant variables have been accounted for, there remains a sizeable "unexplained residual". This is the case even when the aggregates considered are very large, and is then due to the lack of independence in the fluctuations of men's behavior, as between individuals ("imitation", "infection", "fashion").

Though exemplified in particular behavior relations, viz; those explaining the demand for cash, the discussion of Lectures 5, 6, 7 was intended to apply also to other relations which will play a role in the course.

---

* In more specific terms: to derive the aggregate equation (7.3) from the micro-equation (7.1) it is not sufficient to know the n probability distributions (7.2) referring to each of the n individuals. It is necessary to know the "joint probability distribution"; e.g., to know the probability that a certain deviation (say, -1) of the first individual is accompanied by specified deviations of the second, third,...n-th individual. Or, in terms of "statistical parameters": even if each single distribution such as (7.2) could be completely described by its standard deviation, we need also know the correlation coefficients for each pair of individuals.

Lecture 8: EFFECT OF (EXOGENOUS) INVESTMENT UPON NATIONAL INCOME: A DYNAMIC MODEL

The models of Lectures 2-4 are *static*. That is, they cannot explain the chain of events in time except through changes in external variables. For example, if the external variables (parameters) $\bar{I}$, α_0, α_1, in (3.1.B), (3.2.B), (3.3.B) are fixed at certain levels, then certain values of the three economic variables, Y, C, I satisfy those three conditions. These values are called the "solution(s)" and depend on the external variables only:

(8.A) $Y = (\bar{I} + \alpha_0)/(1 - \alpha_1)$ [cf. (3.4.B)]

(8.B) $C = (\alpha_1\bar{I} + \alpha_0)/(1 - \alpha_1)$

(8.C) $I = \bar{I}$

If $\bar{I}$ is replaced by a new value, $\bar{I} + \Delta\bar{I}$, while α_0, α_1 remain unchanged, Y will also change, viz., by the amount

$\Delta\bar{I}/(1 - \alpha_1)$.

(Similarly one can derive the effect of a change in α_1).

But the transition of Y from its old to its new level can be explained only in a *dynamic* model: a model in which at least one of the internal variables enters at two distinct points of time, thus linking the past and the present, the present and the future. Replace, for example, the system (3.1), (3.2), (3.3) by

(8.1) $C_t = \alpha(Y_t)$; (8.2) $I_t = \bar{I}_t$; (8.3) $Y_{t+\theta} = C_t + \bar{I}_t$,

where t indicates time (e.g., Y_t = annual rate of income at time point t), and θ is the time-lag in the businessmen's reaction. This lag is due to psychology as well as technology. If this lag is negligible, (3.3) becomes a tolerable approximation of the more realistic (8.3). In this case, the variables Y, C are (almost) constant through time as long as $\bar{I}_t$ and the function $\alpha(\ \ )$ are constant. But if θ is sizeable, Y and C change even if the external variables are fixed. We have, by substituting (8.1) and (8.2) into (8.3)

(8.4) $Y_{t+\theta} = \alpha(Y_t) + \bar{I}_t$:

thus income at any time will depend on an earlier income, but will not, in general be equal to it. To give a "*solution*" for Y means now, not to give a certain constant value for Y but to construct the *path* of Y_t through time, beginning with a given initial value Y_0. Such construction is possible, by (8.4): $Y_1 = \alpha(Y_0) + \bar{I}_1$; $Y_2 = \alpha(Y_1) + \bar{I}_2$; etc..... The path will depend on the function α and on the externally prescribed path of $\bar{I}$.

In the particular case of a *stable* dynamic model each variable converges to some constant value as time goes on. If our dynamic model (8.1), (8.2), (8.3) is stable, the differences $(Y_{t+\theta} - Y_t)$, $(C_{t+\theta} - C_t)$ converge to zero as times goes on ("as $t \to \infty$"). If we denote the "equilibrium values", i.e., the constants to which Y, C converge, by Y_∞, C_∞, and the externally fixed value of I by $\bar{I}$, then (8.3) implies

$$(8.5)\quad Y_\infty = C_\infty + \bar{I},$$

since as time goes on, the error of replacing $Y_{t+\theta}$ by Y_t tends to vanish. We recognize in (8.5) the "equilibrium condition " (3.3)--now properly specified as being valid "in the long run" only.

As an example of a stable dynamic model, assume the linear consumption function as in (3.-1.B), restricted by the condition

$$(8.6)\quad 0 < \alpha_1 < 1 \qquad [\text{cf. } (4.1)]$$

This example will illustrate the "dynamic theory of the multiplier". (8.4) becomes

$$(8.7)\quad Y_{t+\theta} = \alpha_1 Y_t + \alpha_0 + I_t$$

Suppose that until time t = 0 investment was fixed at I_0 and the system was in equilibrium, so that $Y_0 = Y_{-\theta}$. That is, by (8.7) and denoting $I_0 + \alpha_0$ by γ,

$$(8.8.0)\quad Y_0 = \alpha_1 Y_0 + \alpha_0 + I_0 = \alpha_1 Y_0 + \gamma.$$

Suppose that at time t = 0, investment is raised by 1 unit and remains at this new level indefinitely; then, by (8.7)

$$(8.8.1)\quad Y_\theta = \alpha_1 Y_0 + \alpha_0 + I_0 + 1 = \alpha_1 Y_0 + \gamma + 1$$

$$= [\text{by } (8.8.0)]\ Y_0 + 1$$

$$(8.8.2)\quad Y_{2\theta} = \alpha_1 Y_\theta + \gamma + 1 = \alpha_1(Y_0 + 1) + \gamma + 1 = Y_0 + 1 + \alpha_1$$

$$(8.8.3)\quad Y_{3\theta} = Y_0 + 1 + \alpha_1 + \alpha_1^2, \text{ etc.}$$

. . . .

$$(8.8.\infty)\quad Y_\infty = Y_0 + 1/(1 - \alpha_1).$$

Thus differences between successive income levels are $1, \alpha_1, \alpha_1^2, \ldots$ converging to zero as time goes on, since, by (8.6), α_1 was assumed to be a proper fraction. We can represent the process graphically as a race between the income (or supply) Y_t and demand $D_t = \alpha_1 Y_{t-\theta} + \gamma + 1$ The excess demand $D_t - Y_t$ is zero initially, is raised to 1 at time 0, and diminishes progressively as both D_t and Y_t converge to a new equilibrium value which is $1/(1 - \alpha_1)$ above the initial one. On Graph 8:I, $\alpha_1 = 2/3$.

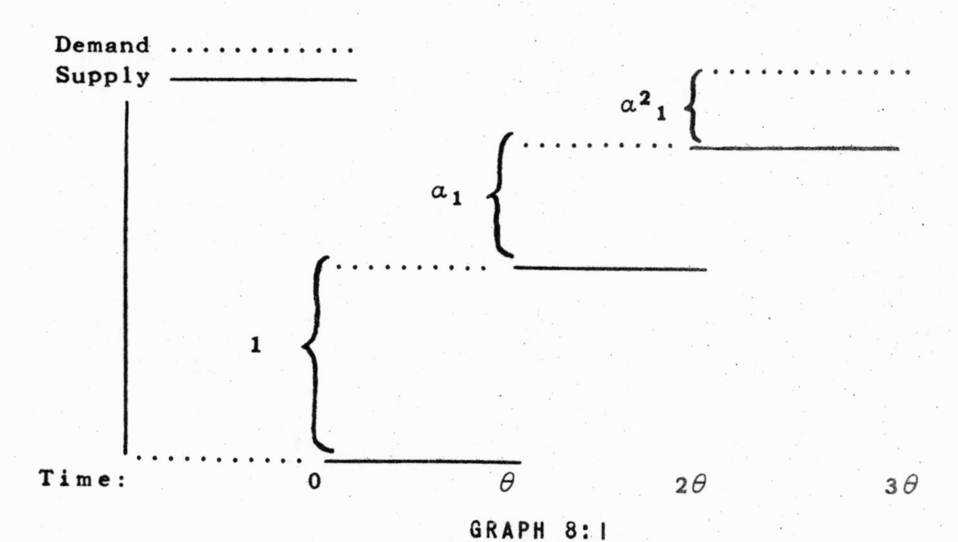

GRAPH 8:1

RACE BETWEEN DEMAND AND SUPPLY (IN DOLLARS PER YEAR) WHEN $a_1 = 2/3$ AND INVESTMENT IS FIXED AT 1 UNIT ABOVE ITS INITIAL LEVEL.

Lecture 9: COMPARATIVE STATICS AND DYNAMICS. CONCEPTS OF STABILITY.

Another geometrical representation (reminiscent of that of the "cobweb theorem") uses the static framework of Graph 4:I where Q denotes the initial, and R the final equilibrium combinations of Demand and Supply, and where Q', Q", Q''' ... are intermediate **positions.**

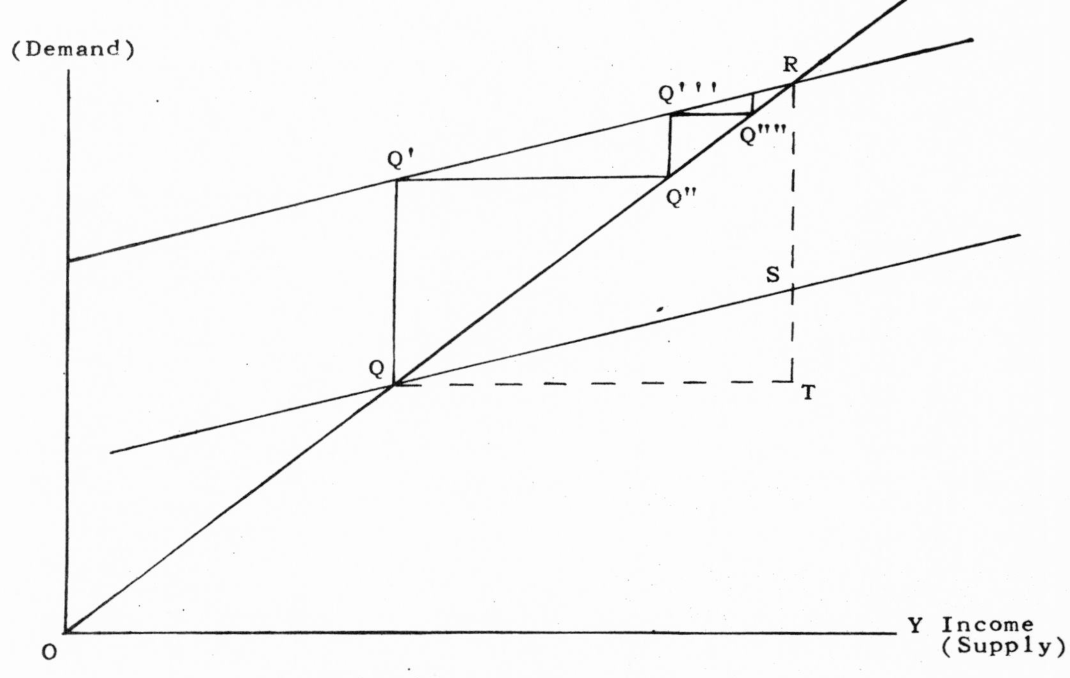

GRAPH 9:I *(Compare GRAPH 4:I)*

(slope SQT = α_1; slope ROY = 1; QQ' = change in investment; QT = ultimate change in income.)

In Lecture 8, we assumed a time lag in the behavior of producers only: θ time units elapse between Q' and Q", again between Q''' and Q"". But the **jump** from Q" to Q''' (change in demand in response to higher income payments to workers and others) is instantaneous. We can now introduce a time-lag for consumers also: say, θ' time units between income raise and the rise in demand for consumers' goods (difference between positions Q" and Q'''). The model becomes

(9.1) $C_t = \alpha(Y_{t-\theta'})$	(9.1.L) $C_t = \alpha_1 Y_{t-\theta'} + \alpha_0$
(9.2) $I_t = \bar{I}_t$	(9.2.L) $I_t = \bar{I}_t$
(9.3) $Y_{t+\theta} = C_t + I_t$	(9.3.L) $Y_{t+\theta} = C_t + I_t$

Income at any time is therefore derivable from earlier income by the relation

$$(9.4)\ Y_{t+\theta} = \alpha(Y_{t-\theta'}) + \bar{I}_t \qquad (9.4.L)\ Y_{t+\theta} = \alpha_1 Y_{t-\theta'} + \alpha_0 + \bar{I}_t$$

In the linear case, we can also write

$$(9.5)\ Y_{t+\theta+\theta'} = \alpha_1 Y_t + \alpha_0 + \bar{I}_{t+\theta'}$$

This is similar to (8.7): income at any time depends on lagged income and on lagged investment; but income is now lagged by $\theta + \theta'$, i.e., the delays in production and consumption are added. The solution, i.e., the path of Y through time is similar to that of Lecture 8; the equilibrium value is exactly the same but successive increases of Y by 1, α_1, α_1^2, etc., are **separated by a longer time.**

The comparison of the two models, $\theta' = 0$ (Lecture 8) and $\theta' > 0$ (present lecture) is a typical problem in *comparative dynamics*. In Lecture 1, problems in *comparative statics* were formulated; to measure the effect of the change in a (controlled or non-controlled parameter of a static model upon the values of the economic variables, i.e., upon the "solution", of the static model. Analogously, comparative dynamics studies the effect of a change in a parameter of the model (such as θ) upon the "solution", i.e., upon the path (or "time-shape") of each economic variable. The path itself is characterized by certain parameters, e.g., the equilibrium value (if the model is stable, as ours is); the time-distance between steps (if such steps can be defined, as is the case with our model), etc. If the path were "cyclical", i.e., showed periodicity, the length of each wave would be another important path-parameter. Comparative dynamics, then, studies the effect of a change in a given parameter of the system upon each of the important parameters of the path; and the matrix I.2 can be re-labelled accordingly. Problems in business cycles policy are of this nature; we want to know how a change in policy (i.e., in a controlled parameter) affects, say, the time-length of the cycle.

In every dynamic model of this and the preceding lecture, restoration of equilibrium takes "infinite time". The duration of full adjustment could not therefore be used as a path-parameter. Instead one can ask: How long does it take to achieve one-half--or 75%, 90%, or any preassigned fraction k--of the adjustment? The final gain in income in response to a unit increase in investment is the difference

$$Y_\infty - Y_0 = 1/(1 - \alpha_1);$$

an intermediate income gain--say, at time of the n-th step, i.e., $n(\theta + \theta')$ time units after the disturbance, is

$$1 + \alpha_1 + \alpha_1^2 + \ldots + \alpha_1^{n-1} = (1 - \alpha_1^n) / (1 - \alpha_1).$$

The ratio between the intermediate and the final gain is, therefore, $1 - \alpha_1^n$.

We ask what is the "half-life" (or "75%-life", "90%-life") of the adjustment. Put

$$1 - \alpha_1^n = 1/2 \text{ (or 75\%, 90\% . . .), hence}$$

$$\alpha_1^n = 1/2 \text{ (or 25\%, 10\% . . .).}$$

We find, for example, that if $\alpha_1 = 3/4$, three steps achieve half of adjustment, since $(3/4)^2 = 9/16$, $(3/4)^3 < 1/2$. The needed number of steps is the smaller, the *smaller* α_1 (and hence the smaller the multiplier). Therefore, the increase in α_1 (e.g., through transfer of income of the rich to the poor) is *not* conducive to "stability" of the system if the degree of stability is defined as the period necessary to achieve a given fraction of adjustment. (Or: "necessary to overcome a given fraction of the disturbance", the disturbance being measured as the difference between demand and supply, $D_t - Y_t$: see Graph 8:I).

Obviously, an increase in one or both of the lags (θ or θ') has also a "destabilizing" effect in the sense just defined.

QUESTION: Comment on the following statement: "Both the velocity of circulation, $v = Y/M$, and the multiplier, $\partial Y/\partial I$, turn out to lie around 3. This suggests that they are identical. In fact, the effect of a change in investment works out in the following steps: additional money is paid out to workers and others; it is spent by them $1/v$ time units later, thus creating new demand for labor and other factors of production, etc. The greater v, the larger the effect of given investment."

COMMENT. (1) The two quantities cannot be identical; v is measured in "times per year", while the multiplier is a pure number. (2) However, the time-length $1/v$ would be partly reflected in lag θ' if consumers would revise their purchases not at the time of the revision of their income contracts (e.g., being hired, or being granted higher wages) but at the time of receiving cash. The time-path of Y is then affected by a change in v--not in the sense that Y_∞ and the multiplier, $\partial Y/\partial I$, are changed--but in the sense that the duration of each adjustment step, $\theta + \theta'$, and therefore the "half-life" of adjustment is changed. (3) Accordingly, the velocity of circulation would enter the model as a parameter of two independent equations: the demand for cash equation (with interest r as a further variable)

$$(9.6) \quad M = \lambda(Y, r; v)$$

and the consumption equation

$$(9.7) \quad C = \alpha(Y_{t-\theta'(v)});$$

the function $\theta'(\ )$ indicating the way in which a change in v affects the lag between income and consumption.

Lecture 10: AGGREGATION OF INDIVIDUAL CONSUMPTION FUNCTIONS

As an example of aggregation, Problem 2 was discussed: "Using Table 308, Statistical Abstract 1947, estimate the relationship between per-family income and per-family consumption if the changes in the income of each family obey one of the following conditions:

(10.A) All incomes change by the same amount of dollars;

(10.B) All incomes change by the same percentage."

The demand of a single family for consumption goods (in dollars) was assumed to be a function of this family's money income only ("personal consumption function"):

(10.1) $C_\nu = \alpha^*(Y_\nu)$, $\nu = 1, \ldots, n$

The relation to be derived is that between per-family (or average) consumption demand, C, and per-family (or average) money income Y; the "collective consumption function":

(10.2) $C = \alpha(Y)$,

where $C = \frac{1}{n}\Sigma_\nu C_\nu$, $Y = \frac{1}{n}\Sigma_\nu Y_\nu$.

It was made clear that hypotheses alternative to (10.1) were excluded, for example, the following hypotheses,

(10.1.1) $C_{\nu,\tau} = \alpha^*(Y_{\nu,\tau}, Y_{\nu,\tau-\theta})$, where θ is a lag;

(10.1.2) $C_{\nu,\tau} = \alpha^*(Y_{\nu,\tau}, Y^0_{\nu,\tau})$, where $Y^0_{\nu,\tau}$ is the highest income reached at any time before τ. (Modigliani)

Thus (10.1.1) expresses the slowness of adjustment of consumption both upward and downward; while (10.1.2) expresses the slowness of people's adjustment downward, to new poverty. Appropriate combinations of these hypotheses could be devised. Also, (10.1.2) could be amplified to include as a further variable the time elapsed since the last peak of income.

These refinements were excluded from consideration. Excluded also was the fact that, given the income, consumption depends on the size of the family. It was understood that having two (or three, four, ...) instead of one independent variable in (10.1) would require data in a form different from the simple "single entry" table of the Statistical Abstract, which gives consumption and relative frequencies for each bracket of current income. The hypothesis (10.1.1), for example, would require a double-entry table, showing the consumption and the relative frequency for each "cell" corresponding to a given current and given past income-bracket.

To fix the ideas, assume (10.1) to be a quadratic:

$$(10.3)\ C_\nu = \alpha_0 + \alpha_1 Y_\nu + \alpha_2 Y_\nu{}^2 = \alpha^*(Y_\nu);$$

then, by the definitions of the averages, C and Y, we have

$$(10.4)\ C = \alpha_0 + \alpha_1 Y + \alpha_2 \cdot \frac{1}{n}\Sigma Y_\nu{}^2 = \alpha(Y);$$

now define the variance (= square of standard deviation) of family incomes

$$(10.5)\ \sigma^2 = \frac{1}{n}\Sigma(Y_\nu - Y)^2;$$

it obeys an identity taught in elementary statistics:

$$\frac{1}{n}\Sigma Y_\nu{}^2 = Y^2 + \sigma^2$$

Hence (10.4) becomes

$$C = \alpha_0 + \alpha_1 Y + \alpha_2 Y^2 + \alpha_2 \sigma^2$$

$$(10.6)\ \alpha(Y) = \alpha^*(Y) + \alpha_2 \sigma^2$$

If the "personal consumption function" $\alpha^*(\ \ )$ is a straight line, then α_2 in (10.3) vanishes; and (10.6) shows that in this case, the personal and the collective consumption functions coincide. This also follows, of course, directly by forming averages on both sides of the equation

$$C_\nu = \alpha_0 + \alpha_1 Y_\nu;$$

$$C = \alpha_0 + \alpha_1 Y$$

In this case no transfer of money between poor and rich has any effect upon average (and therefore total) consumption as long as the total (and therefore average) income, Y, remains the same. This is obvious, since, in this case, the transfer of a dollar reduces the consumption of the rich man by, say, 1/2 dollar, and increases the consumption of the poor by exactly the same amount. (Note that the linearity of consumption function means that the *marginal*, but not necessarily the *average* propensity to consume is independent of income! We have, in general, $\alpha_0 > 0$: The rich may consume a smaller proportion of their income than the poor do of theirs. The relevant question is whether they consume a smaller proportion of any added, or subtracted, income.)

In general, α_2 is not zero, but presumably *negative*: The function $\alpha^*(\ \ )$ is convex with respect to the C axis, i.e., the slope, or marginal propensity, falls as income rises. (10.6) implies, therefore, that $\alpha(Y)$ lies below $\alpha^*(Y)$; that is, for any Y,

$$(10.8)\ \alpha(Y) < \alpha^*(Y)$$

It will be shown in Lecture 11 that this result is general, for any convex curve $\alpha^*(Y)$, and not only a quadratic one. We also see immediately that, quite generally, if personal marginal propensity to consume is the smaller the larger the income, then income-equalization raises consumption: The transfer of $1 from a man with 0.5 marginal propensity to consume to a man with 0.8 marginal propensity to consume causes 30¢ increase of consumption. See Graph 10.I.

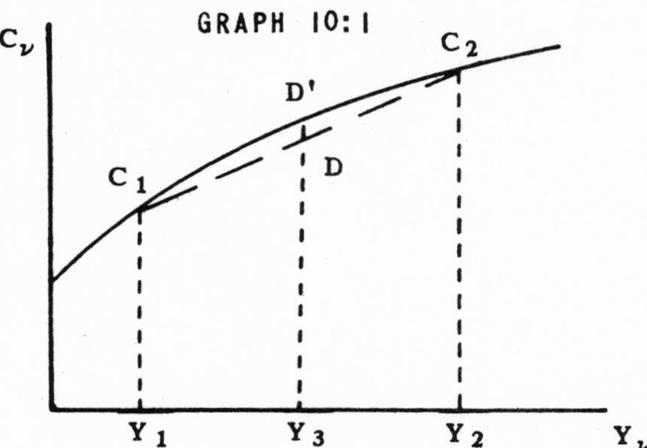

(Effect of income-equalization upon consumption. Average consumption of two families ($\nu = 1, 2$) is, before equalization,

$\overline{Y_3D} = (\overline{Y_1C_1} + \overline{Y_2C_2})/2$, where $Y_3 = (Y_1 + Y_2)/2$.

After equalization, the average consumption is $\overline{Y_3D'}$.

We have $\overline{Y_3D'} > \overline{Y_3D}$ if the curve is convex; $\overline{Y_3D'} = \overline{Y_3D}$ if it is linear.)

Lecture 11: CONTINUATION OF LECTURE 10

Other properties of the collective consumption function $\alpha(\ \ )$, given the personal consumption function $\alpha^*(\ \ )$, depend on what assumptions are made about the way in which income-distribution changes as Y changes. For example, our alternative assumptions (10.A), (10.B) are two such ways.

NOTE: In the economists' language, case (10.B) is one of "unchanged distribution"; for the statistician, distribution is defined by the relative frequencies assigned to the variable--in this case to income--and therefore it changes in case (10.B) as well as (10.A). Case (10.B) might be called that of "constant proportionate shares". In both cases, one distribution parameter, *viz.*, the average (Y) changes. But in case (10.A) the variance σ^2 [defined in (10.5)] is unchanged since, for any family ν, the deviation of its income from the average, $Y_\nu - Y$, is unchanged. In case (10.B), an unchanging character for each family is its relative deviation, $(Y_\nu - Y)/Y$; consequently, the "coefficient of variation" (squared here for convenience),

$$(11.1)\quad (1/n)\Sigma(Y_\nu - Y)^2/Y^2 = \sigma^2/Y^2 = v^2,$$

is unchanged as Y changes.

By (10.6), the (quadratic) personal consumption function lies above its collective counterpart, the distance being $\alpha_2\sigma^2$. This distance is constant in case (10.A). In case (10.B), this distance grows with Y, since $\sigma^2 = v^2Y^2$ and since, in this case, v^2 is constant.

GRAPH 11:1

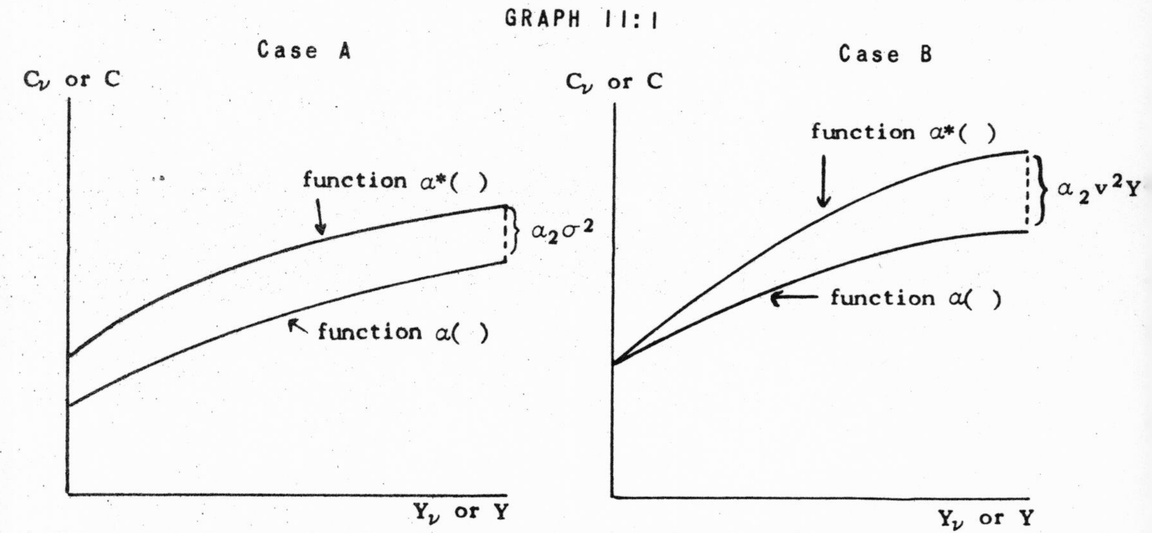

[In each of these two graphs, the upper line represents a (quadratic) personal consumption function, and the lower line, the collective consumption function. A change in average income Y is accompanied, in case A, by equal dollar increments for each family; in case B, by equal percentage increments for each family.]

To assume a quadratic personal consumption function (10.3) and to assume that either the variance or the coefficient of variation are kept constant while average income changes [cases (10.A), (10.B) respectively], is at best an approximation which serves to illustrate the relation between micro- and macroeconomics. For further discussion see 1) "Consumer Expenditures in U.S.", National Resources Committee, 1939, Appendix C; 2) J. Marschak, "Personal and Collective Budget Functions", Review of Economic Statistics, 1939.

However, the inequality (10.8) does not depend on those special assumptions, provided the personal marginal propensity to consume does decrease with income, i.e., $\alpha^*(\ \ )$ is convex with respect to the C-axis. Given any income distribution, the average income Y can be regarded as marked by the center of gravity of points on the Y_ν-axis, the axis being conceived as a wire having different density at different parts (corresponding to the different relative frequencies at different income brackets). Similarly, the average consumption C can be regarded as the center of gravity of points on the C_ν-axis. Consequently, the point (C,Y) is the center of gravity of the curved wire representing the equation $C_\nu = \alpha^*(Y_\nu)$; and, with that curve convex, the center of gravity will lie "inside", and therefore below it (Graph 11:II). If the distribution (of densities, i.e., of income-frequencies) is changed in some prescribed way, the center of gravity will shift, tracing out the $\alpha(Y)$-curve (possibly with loops, etc.), which will lie below the $\alpha^*(Y_\nu)$ curve.

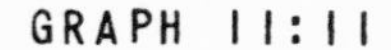
GRAPH 11:II

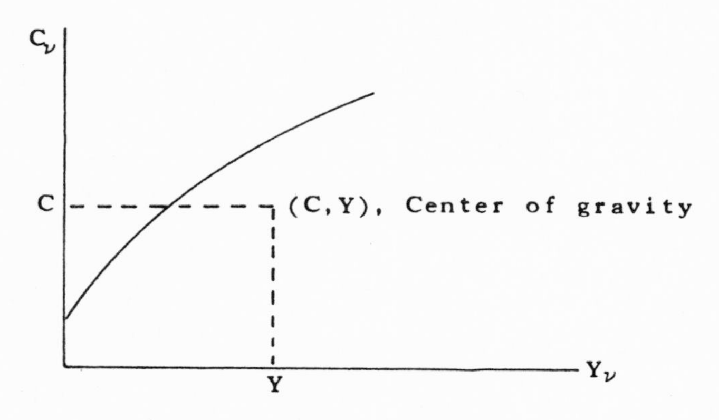

Lecture 12: EFFECT OF GOVERNMENT EXPENDITURES AND TAXES UPON NATIONAL INCOME

The sample data used in Problem 2 gave the relation between family consumption and the *disposable* income (= income after personal taxes), and consequently the collective consumption function derived from it should be written, in the notation of the earlier lectures:

$$(12)\quad C = \alpha(Y - T),$$

where $\alpha(\ \ )$ is a function, Y is per-family income after taxes, and T is the government's tax receipts per family. (We shall disregard all other than personal taxes). Since we consider population as given, all that follows can be easily translated into terms of total consumption, total income, total tax-receipts instead of the per-family quantities, provided the function $\alpha(\ \ )$ is given. Throughout the rest of the course, we shall deal with totals, unless stated otherwise.

Denote by G the government expenditure, while I will be, from now on, used to denote the private net investment only. If we assume I, G, and T exogenous, and assume the consumption function linear over the relevant interval, the system of Lecture 3 becomes:

$$(12.1)\quad C = \alpha_0 + \alpha_1(Y - T)$$

$$(12.2)\quad Y = C + I + G,$$

$$(12.3\text{-}5)\quad I = \overline{I},\ G = \overline{G},\ T = \overline{T},$$

but instead of writing out the last three equations we can note verbally that I, G, T are exogenous, i.e., given and independent of the other variables of the system, and thus spare the symbols $\overline{I}$, $\overline{G}$, $\overline{T}$. We can solve (12.1) and (12.2), i.e., express Y and C in terms of the givens:

$$(12.6)\quad Y = \frac{I + G + \alpha_0}{1 - \alpha_1} - \frac{\alpha_1}{1 - \alpha_1}T.$$

We note that the "government expenditure multiplier"

$$(12.7)\quad \frac{\partial Y}{\partial G} = \frac{\partial Y}{\partial I} = \frac{1}{1 - \alpha_1}\ (\text{e.g., } = 3 \text{ if } \alpha_1 = 2/3,)$$

while the "tax-receipts multiplier"

$$(12.8)\quad \frac{\partial Y}{\partial T} = -\frac{\alpha_1}{1 - \alpha_1}\ (\text{e.g., } = -2 \text{ if } \alpha_1 = 2/3).$$

Thus if government expenditure is increased by ΔG, (say \$4 billion) while tax receipts are increased by ΔT, (say, \$1 billion), the income increment is:

$$\Delta Y = \frac{\partial Y}{\partial G} \cdot \Delta G + \frac{\partial Y}{\partial T} \cdot \Delta T;$$

$= (3 \times 4) - (2 \times 1)$ (if $\alpha_1 = 2/3$) = \$10 billion.

If the increase in government expenditure is fully balanced by an increase in taxes, i.e., if both are increased by ΔG, then

$$(12.9)\quad \Delta Y = \frac{1}{1 - \alpha_1} \cdot \Delta G - \frac{\alpha_1}{1 - \alpha_1} \Delta G = \Delta G,$$

that is, income increases by \$1 for each dollar increase in tax-financed government expenditure. This result has nothing to do with the redistributive effect of progressive taxes, or of certain types of public works. It would hold also if the taxes were proportionate; or if all incomes were equal; or if the personal consumption function were linear (making--as shown in Lecture 10--total consumption independent of income distribution). The result (12.9) appears less paradoxical if one remembers that the government increases its demand by the full amount of tax, while the consumers diminish their demand by only a fraction α_1 of the tax. Consider successive steps ("dynamic approach": Lectures 8-9):

Adding \$1 to tax receipts changes demand by: $-\alpha_1 - \alpha_1^2 - \alpha_1^3 - \ldots$

Adding \$1 to goverment expenditure changes demand by: $+1 + \alpha_1 + \alpha_1^2 + \ldots$,

Cancelling $-\alpha_1$ and $+\alpha_1$, $-\alpha_1^2$ and $+\alpha_1^2$, etc., we obtain a net total of \$1.

Different results are obtained if I or G or T are not exogenous. For example, it is claimed that entrepreneurs may be "scared" by government expenditure into an "investment strike": say,

$$(12.3.a)\quad I = \beta_0 - \beta_1 G \qquad (\beta_1 > 0):$$

inserting this into (12.6) we have

$$(12.6.a)\quad Y = \frac{G(1 - \beta_1) + \alpha_0 + \beta_0}{1 - \alpha_1} - \frac{\alpha_1}{1 - \alpha_1} T:$$

in this case the multiplier of government spending is

$$(12.7.a)\quad \frac{\partial Y}{\partial G} = \frac{1 - \beta_1}{1 - \alpha_1}$$

and is smaller than when I is exogenous, as was the case in (12.7). Other hypotheses about non-exogenous investment will be studied later.

It is certain that T is not exogenous: the government fixes the *tax-schedule* (a functional relationship between individual income and tax), not the *tax-receipts*. As a simple example, assume a proportional income tax, hence

$$T = Y \cdot \tau,$$

where τ means "tax-rate". Instead of (12.1) we then have

$$(12.1.b)\quad C = \alpha_0 + \alpha_1(1 - \tau)Y$$
$$= \alpha_0 + \alpha_1{}'Y,$$

where $\alpha_1{}' = \alpha_1(1 - \tau)$ can be called the "net marginal propensity to consume". (12.6) becomes

$$(12.6.b)\quad Y = \frac{I + G + \alpha_0}{1 - \alpha_1{}'} .$$

An increase in tax-rate is thus equivalent to a certain decrease in the multiplier.

We can ask two questions:

1) What is the effect of tax-rate increase upon equilibrium income, given the level of investment and government spending: obviously

$$(12.8)\quad \frac{\partial Y}{\partial \tau} < 0, \text{ since } \frac{\partial Y}{\partial \alpha_1{}'} > 0.$$

In this sense, tax-rate increase is "deflationary" (and not "inflationary").

2) What is the effect of tax-rate increase upon the multiplier, i.e., upon $\partial Y/\partial G$, i.e., upon the size of income change produced by a given change in government spending (or investment). As already remarked, the multiplier is the larger, the larger $\alpha_1{}'$, i.e., the smaller τ:

$$(12.9)\quad \frac{\partial}{\partial \tau}\left(\frac{\partial Y}{\partial G}\right) < 0.$$

In this sense, an increase in tax-rate is "stabilizing" (and not "de-stabilizing").

Lecture 13: NON-EXOGENOUS INVESTMENT

As a step to make the model of Lecture 3 more realistic, we drop the assumption that investment is exogenous. In the version of the "Washington-Keynesian" model, investment depends on national income. A vague reason for this may be that entrepreneurs decide to enlarge plant if they expect high future sales or high future profits; that high future profits or sales are expected when current profits or sales are high; and that current profits and sales are strongly correlated with national income. However, precisely what causes the firm executive to expect high profits (say), how this expectation moves him to choose a particular investment level and how such individual responses are to be aggregated into a macroeconomic relation, we shall not attempt to analyze here. (In the case of consumption, the aggregation step was explained in some detail in Lectures 10-11, but the preceding steps--*e.g.*, deriving the personal consumption function from the principle of utility maximization--were also not attempted.) We have, then

(13.1) $C = \alpha(Y)$	or, in	(13.1.L) $C = \alpha_0 + \alpha_1 Y$
(13.2) $I = \beta(Y)$	parti-	(13.2.L) $I = \beta_0 + \beta_1 Y$
(13.3) $Y = C + I + G$	cular,	(13.3.L) $Y = C + I + G$;

the exogenous variable G will here indicate deficit-financed government expenditure; we neglect taxes to simplify the presentation --but they could be easily introduced on the lines of Lecture 12.

If we denote C + I by D (for private demand), and the sum of functions $\alpha(Y) + \beta(Y)$ by a function $\delta(Y)$ ("Propensity to spend function"), or--in the linear case--with $\alpha_0 + \beta_0 = \delta_0$ and $\alpha_1 + \beta_1 = \delta_1$ ("marginal propensity to consume *and* invest), we have again a two-equations model

(13.4) $D = \delta(Y)$	or	(13.4.L) $D = \delta_0 + \delta_1 Y$
(13.5) $Y = D + G$		(13.5.L) $Y = D + G$.

It follows that $Y = (\delta_0 + G)/(1 - \delta_1)$; "the multiplier" $= 1/(1 - \delta_1)$.

Graphs 4:I and 9:I are applicable to our new system with appropriate changes: instead of drawing the line $\alpha(Y)$ and shifting it by a given amount of investment (which included government demand), we now draw the line $\delta(Y)$ and shift it by the amount of government demand. Note that if G = 0, we have

(13.6) $D = \delta(Y)$	or	(13.6.L) $D = \delta_0 + \delta_1 Y$
(13.7) $D = Y$		(13.7.L) $D = Y$

a system of two equations in two variables which has been repeatedly misunderstood in economic literature. The misunderstanding is similar to the one that would arise if, from the condition that demand be equal to supply one would conclude that the demand curve and the supply curve are two identical curves. In our case we also have two distinct curves: one--(13.6)--describes the behavior of demanders and states that total demand changes with income in some particular way; the other--(13.7)--expresses the proposition that demand should equal income. This proposition is sometimes called "equilibrium condition" (we shall discuss the term "equilibrium" in a moment). The point of intersection of the two curves gives that particular pair of values of the two variables (income and demand) at which both conditions are satisfied. It is sometimes stated that the sum of investment and consumption "equals income by definition", or, in other words, "investment is by definition equal to savings". But, on such a definition, investment would not be the same variable as the investment I in (13.2); and we would have only one equation, viz., (13.7).

Along the curve (13.7), the increment of spending is equal to that of income. But along the curve (13.6) the two increments are not equal. It is the ratio of the latter two increments that we call the "marginal propensity to spend" (sum of marginal propensities to consume and to invest). Such is, in the linear case, the coefficient δ_1 in the equation (13.6.L).

Actually, we are not compelled to assume that the equilibrium condition is "always" satisfied. All that the economists have in mind by this condition is, that if equilibrium is absent, then changes must take place till the equilibrium is reached. In other words, (13.7) is a mere approximation of some dynamic statement such as

$$(13.8)\ (Y_t - D_t) \rightarrow 0 \text{ as } t \rightarrow \infty.$$

Thus, equations (13.6.L) and (13.7.L) are quite distinct. From the validity of (13.7.L) it does not follow, not even "in the long-run", that $\delta_Y = 1$, $\delta_0 = 0$! (Analogy: from the requirement that demand be equal supply, it does not follow that the demand curve and the supply curve are identical curves!)

The equilibrium values of economic variables have also been called their "ex-post" values; the term "ex-ante" would then apply to values that are taken by economic variables before the equilibrium has been achieved. It is, of course, the "ex-ante" values that are meant when response equations such as (13.4) are written. Another term for "ex-ante" is "intended". *E.g.*, the quantities plotted on the demand curve or on the supply curve are "intended" quantities; but at one particular price these quantities take values that satisfy the equilibrium condition (*viz.*, the condition that they be equal).

The difference $Y_t - D_t$ in (13.8) has been occasionally called "hoarding" (of money)--an unhappy terminology since it may strongly suggest an increase in the national *stock of money*. There is to be sure, an (unintended) increase in the *stock of goods*. However, this increase may not fully coincide with $Y_t - D_t$ since not all goods are storeable: when the demand for electricity falls short of capacity of power plants, the difference $Y_t - D_t$ shows itself in the continued fixed charges and (usually) not in accumulation of produced electricity. Thus the statement in Lecture 3 that identified $Y_t - D_t$ with "unintended increase in inventories" has to be corrected.

Lecture 14: INTEREST RATE AND THE DEMAND FOR GOODS

Equation (13.2) may be criticized for not including interest rate among the variables affecting the decision to invest. The cheaper a firm can borrow money, the more likely it is to expand it's plant and equipment, given the rate of profits ("the marginal efficiency of capital") that are expected to be yielded by additional plant or equipment. Using linear approximations, with $\beta_r > 0$,

$$(14.1)\quad I = \beta_o - \beta_r r + \beta_y Y,$$

If the interest rate also affects consumption (and saving) decisions, we write

$$(14.2)\quad C = \alpha_o - \alpha_r r + \alpha_y Y.$$

We recognize in α_y the marginal propensity to consume, previously denoted by α_1; we have (see Lecture 4)

$$0 < \alpha_y < 1.$$

As to the sign of α_r, the effect of interest rate upon consumption, "impatience" (preferring consumption in the present to consumption in the future) would suggest that $\alpha_r > 0$. On the other hand, as pointed out long ago by Marshall, Carver, and others, $\alpha_r < 0$ if society consists of people who plan to save, in the course of their active life, a fixed total sum. The higher the interest rate, the smaller the annual saving (*e.g.*, life insurance premiums) needed to compound a fixed desired total. Finally, a large class of consumers is probably indifferent to interest rate (making $|\alpha_r|$ approach zero) at least as long as the interest rate has the low levels characteristic of Western civilization in the last hundred years or more. Empirical evidence collected by Paul H. Douglas and by E. A. Radice suggests that, for the aggregate of consumers in the U.S.A. or Great Britain, α_r is near zero. It is almost certainly smaller in absolute value than β_r.

Businessmen when questioned by economists (of Oxford and of Harvard around 1938) have often stated that the interest rate plays too small a part in their cost to affect their investment plans, although this would not be true of the residential building industry which contributes a large share of total investment of the nation.

On the balance, the sum $\alpha_r + \beta_r$ is probably positive, though much further research, including surveys of businessmen's attitudes, is needed. For further discussion of our model, it is this sum,

$$\delta_r = \alpha_r + \beta_r > 0,$$

that will matter. Denote total private (*i.e.*, non-governmental) demand by D and write

$$D = I + C;\ \delta_o = \alpha_o + \beta_o;\ \delta_y = \alpha_y + \beta_y;\ \delta_r = \alpha_r + \beta_r,$$

so that (14.1), (14.2) become

$$(14.3)\ D = \delta_o - \delta_r r + \delta_y Y$$

where δ_o, δ_r, δ_y are all positive.

Note that in (14.1) and (14.2)--and therefore also in (14.3)--we have neglected taxes. On the lines of Lecture 12, we ought to replace income Y by the disposable income of individuals and of firms, thus introducing the exogenous variable T (tax revenue) or, better, τ (tax-rate). But different tax receipts and rates would be relevant to the demand of consumers and to that of firms. We don't want to go into detail here, and since the general method of studying the tax effect has been discussed in Lecture 12, we now permit ourselves to neglect taxes altogether and to uphold (14.3).

As before, we have the equilibrium condition for the market of goods: total (private and governmental) demand D + G equals total supply Y:

$$(14.4)\ D + G = Y.$$

Since we have neglected taxes, *i.e.*, put T = 0, the symbol G stands at the same time for government demand and government "deficit-spending". It would not be difficult to re-introduce taxation into the system.

Lecture 15: THE MONEY MARKET

With a new variable (the interest rate, r) now introduced into the system, an additional equation is needed, unless r is exogenous, *i.e.*, determined outside the system. The latter would be the case if the interest rate were directly controlled by the government. We would then write

(15.1) $r = \overline{r}$,

where r is a constant; or we would indicate verbally that r is exogenous. It is somewhat more realistic to describe our monetary institutions by saying that:

(1) public authorities (the Federal Reserve System in vague cooperation with the Treasury Department, directed by the President and loosely supervised by Congress) determine the supply of money, M^s,

(15.1) $M^s = \overline{M}$ (say)

(2) firms and consumers desire to keep aggregate money stocks which are

(a) the larger, the larger their aggregate annual flow of receipts and expenditures, roughly proportional to aggregate income: this is the "transaction motive" for cash holding, the same one that was considered by the classical "circulation velocity" theory (see Lectures 2 and 5) and

(b) the larger, the lower the interest rate. Money's advantage over other assets (durable goods, securities) consists in its costless convertibility into any desirable assets at short notice. If times are uncertain, this advantage is important and is worth the sacrifice of a part of interest receipts. A high interest rate can, however, lure the individual into more daring decisions, *i.e.*, into holding less cash and more securities or durable goods. [On "Money and the Theory of Assets," see Marschak in *Economica* 1938 (with Helen Makower) and in *Econometrica* 1938.] Hence we have the "liquidity preference equation",

(15.2.a) $M^D = \lambda(Y, r)$; (15.2) $M^D = \lambda_o - \lambda_r r + \lambda_y Y$ (using linear approximations) where λ_o, λ_r, λ_y are all positive. The "transaction motive" would account for at least a part of the term $\lambda_y Y$; so that λ_y is roughly equal to or somewhat larger than the "Cambridge k" (= 1/v, the reciprocal of the velocity of circulation).

(3) The demand for money cannot, for any appreciable time, exceed or fall short of money supply:

$$(15.3)\quad M^D = M^s$$

This is an "equilibrium condition" analogous to the one we have met in Lecture 8. Like (8.5), the equation (15.3) is merely an approximation for some dynamic equation that would describe the process which takes place when supply jumps over or dives under the level of demand. Also, institutions are imaginable under which supply for money exceeds demand for a sizable time. This was perhaps the case during the war when durable goods were rationed so that people were forced to hold larger money stocks than they would hold if they had free choice between cash and cars or houses.

We can combine (15.1), (15.2), (15.3) into a single equation

$$(15.4)\quad M = \lambda_o - \lambda_r r + \lambda_y Y$$

and remember that M $(= \overline{M})$ is exogenous.

Lecture 16: EFFECT OF MONEY SUPPLY AND OF GOVERNMENT EXPENDITURES UPON NATIONAL INCOME

The system arrived at in the previous lectures is

(16.1) $D = \delta_o - \delta_r r + \delta_y Y$ [This is (14.3).]

(16.2) $D = Y - G$ [This is (14.4).]

(16.3) $M = \lambda_o - \lambda_r r + \lambda_y Y$ [This is (15.4).]

(16.1) describes decisions on buying; the "equilibrium condition" for the market of goods, (16.2) is an approximation of some dynamic equation stating the response of sellers to excess demand; and (16.3) describes decisions on holding of cash. More precisely, (16.3) is not itself a behavior equation but is already the result of combining the demand-for-cash equation (15.2) with an equilibrium condition for the money market, (15.3). It is then understood that the following quantities in the system are exogenous: M (money supply) and G (government demand for goods, assumed to be financed by deficits only); and the coefficients (the δ's and λ's) are also determined outside of the system. The three endogenous variables are Y, D, and r.

Compare this system of three equations with the two equation-system (13.6), (13.7) of Lecture 13. (16.2) corresponds to (13.7); and (16.1), (16.3) replace the equation (13.6). We have three instead of two equations because we have added a third endogenous variable--the interest rate; G and M are exogenous.

To evaluate the effect of policies (G and M) upon, say, Y, we have to solve the system for Y; that is, to express Y as a function of G and M, and not as a function of other endogenous variables. That is, we have to "eliminate" the other two endogenous variables (D and r). We can do this in two steps:

1) first eliminate D by using (16.1) and (16.2), and obtaining

(16.4) $(1 - \delta_y) \cdot Y + \delta_r \cdot r = G + \delta_o$;

2) then solve (16.4) jointly with (16.3), rewritten as

(16.5) $\lambda_y \cdot Y - \lambda_r \cdot r = M - \lambda_o$.

These two steps are represented on Graphs 16:I, A and B (see next page).

GRAPH 16:1

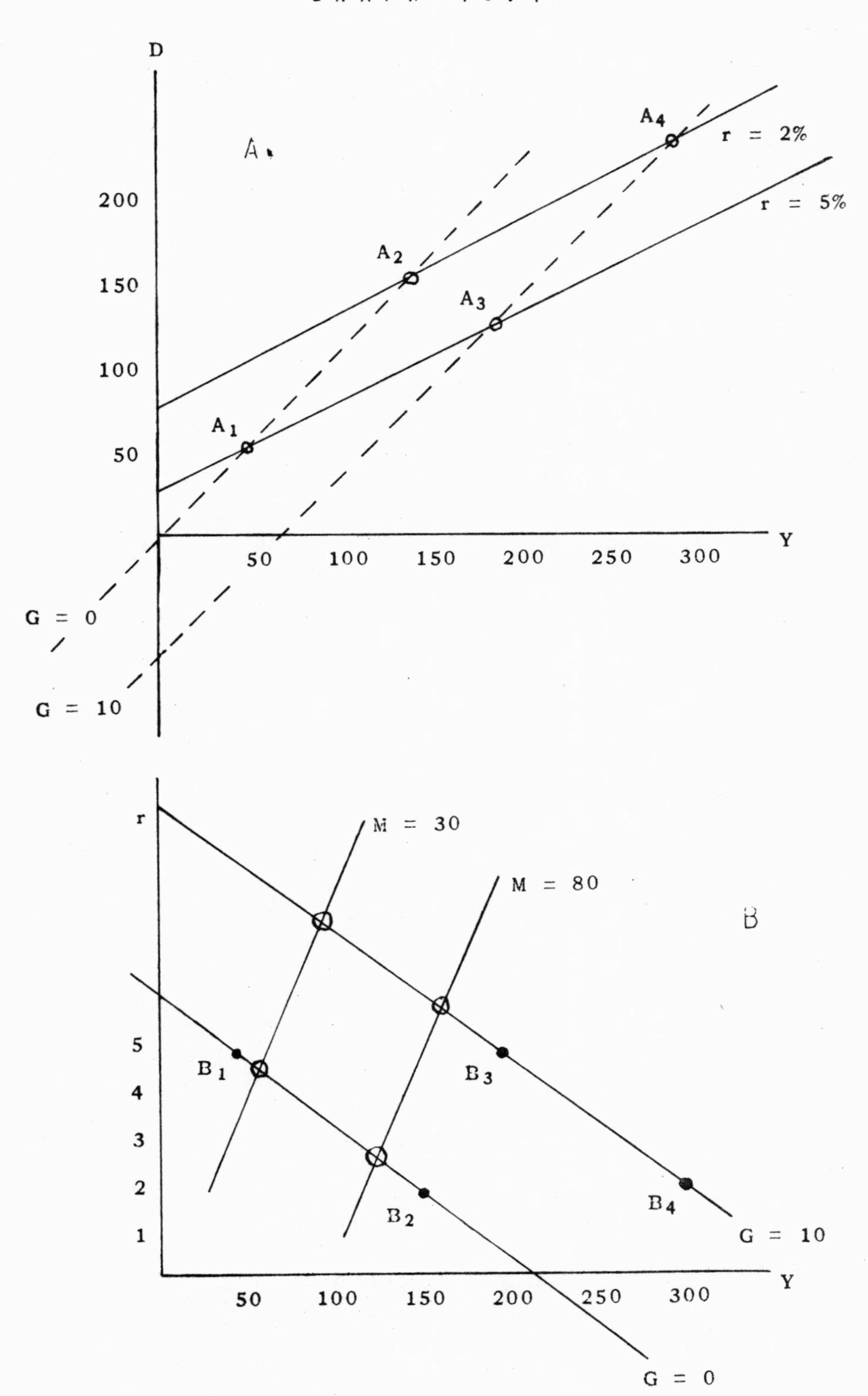
D
A
A4
r = 2%
r = 5%
200
A2
150
A3
100
A1
50
Y
50
100
150
200
250
300
G = 0
G = 10
r
M = 30
M = 80
B
5
B1
B3
4
3
2
B4
B2
1
G = 10
Y
50
100
150
200
250
300
G = 0

Part A of the Graph expresses equation (16.1) as a solid line, for two different levels of interest rate; and equation (16.2) as a dotted line, for two different levels of government deficit. The resulting equilibrium points A_1, A_2, A_3, A_4 are re-plotted on Part B, as points B_1, B_2, B_3, B_4. The negatively sloped lines B_1B_2 and B_3B_4 express equation (16.4) for the two levels of G. The positively sloped lines express equation (16.5) for two different levels of M. Each of the four circled intersection points gives that equilibrium value of Y and r that is generated by each of the four considered pairs of M and G (0 and 30; 0 and 80; 10 and 30; 10 and 80). Algebraically, the joint solution of (16.4) and (16.5) gives

(16.6) $Y = G \cdot (\partial Y/\partial G) + M \cdot (\partial Y/\partial M)$ + a constant term; where

(16.7) $\partial Y/\partial G = \dfrac{\lambda_r}{(1 - \delta_y)\lambda_r + \lambda_y \delta_r}$

(16.8) $\partial Y/\partial M = \dfrac{\delta_r}{(1 - \delta_y)\lambda_r + \lambda_y \delta_r}$, and

(16.9) the constant term $= \dfrac{\lambda_r \delta_o - \lambda_o \delta_r}{(1 - \delta_y)\lambda_r + \lambda_y \delta_r}$.

Unless one is certain that the original equations of the system are linear, the resulting equation (16.6) must not be considered linear, either, except as an approximation. The constant term (16.9) is therefore of little interest. Both the partial derivatives, $\partial Y/\partial G$, $\partial Y/\partial M$ are important even for non-linear systems, provided the changes considered are small. If the increments ΔG and ΔM are small,

(16.10) $\Delta Y = \Delta G \cdot (\partial Y/\partial G) + \Delta M \cdot (\partial Y/\partial M)$.

Similarly, we can solve (16.4), (16.5) with respect to r, and obtain, for the strictly linear case, a solution analogous to (16.6). The important part of the result, valid for small changes also in non-linear cases, is analogous to (16.10):

(16.11) $\Delta r = \Delta G \cdot (\partial r/\partial G) + \Delta M \cdot (\partial r/\partial M)$, where

(16.12) $\partial r/\partial G = \lambda_y$/(a positive denominator)

(16.13) $\partial r/\partial M = -(1 - \delta_y)$/(a positive denominator),

the denominator being the same as in (16.7), (16.8). Thus, a rise in G raises Y as well as r; a rise in M raises Y and depresses r.

(16.7), (16.8), (16.12), (16.13) answer the question: how does a (small) change in each of the two exogenous variables, M and G, affect national income Y and interest rate r. One might also form expressions like $\partial Y/\partial \delta_y$, or $\partial Y/\partial \lambda_r$, etc.: the effect upon income, of a (small) change in the "marginal propensity to demand", or in the "coefficient of liquidity preference", etc.

But it is meaningless (if our model is valid) to ask the question: "What is the effect of a change in the interest rate upon the income," (or "what is the elasticity of income with respect to interest rate"), since both are endogenous. To change any of them, at least one of the exogenous variables, M or G (or one of the Greek letters expressing psychosociological conditions) has to change. If the change in Y and r is due to a change in M only, while G is constant, Y and r move in opposite directions. This is shown by a line such as B_1B_2 or the equation (16.4): the latter equation shows that if G is to be kept constant, an increase in Y must be compensated by a decrease in r. On the other hand, if Y and r change not because of a change in M but because of a change in G, then Y and r move in the same direction: this is clear from (16.5) or from looking at one of the upward sloping lines on Part B of the Graph--say the line labelled "M = 30".

Finally, if both G and M change, then Y and r may move either in the same or in opposite directions (or one may stay unchanged), depending on the size and sign of changes in G and M. The policy instrument may be such as to tie G and M together, for example if deficit is managed by increasing the stock of money. Then, roughly, the increase of the annual deficit by $2 billion a year will increase money stock at the end of the first month by $2/12 billion, at the end of the year by $2 billion, and on the year's average by $1 billion. Therefore, by (16.10), (16.11), income and interest rate will be changed, on the year's average by, respectively

$$\Delta Y = 2 \cdot (\partial Y/\partial G) + (\partial Y/\partial M) \quad \text{and}$$

$$\Delta r = 2 \cdot (\partial r/\partial G) + (\partial r/\partial M).$$

Since the denominators in (16.7), (16.8), (16.12), (16.13), are the same, the ratio between the increments of income and of interest rate is

$$(16.14) \quad \Delta Y/\Delta r = (2\lambda_r + \delta_r)/[2\lambda_y - (1 - \delta_y)].$$

Whether this is positive or negative (i.e., whether Y and r move in the same or opposite directions) depends on whether $2\lambda_y$ is larger or smaller than $(1 - \delta_y)$: i.e., it depends on the way in which demand for cash and demand for goods respond to income changes.

On our Graph (Part B) the tie between changes in G and in M will express itself in the prescription that any shift in the negatively sloped line must be accompanied by a definite (i.e., not an independent) shift in the positively sloped one. Whether the resulting intersection points will align themselves along a positively or a negatively sloped line will then depend on the slopes of the original lines in Parts A and B. This geometrical result remains less definite than the algebraic result (16.14) unless one goes to more trouble.

Another case to consider is that of borrowing from the public. Then M and G could be fixed independently of each other. But this case (analogous to taxes, except when repayment is due), would involve reformulating (16.1) in terms of "disposable" income (see end of Lecture 14). The algebraic analysis of these cases is left to the interested students.

Equations such as (16.6) (and a corresponding one for r) have been called "reduced form". They express each endogenous variable as a function of exogenous variables only, and are therefore useful for discussion of policies. They do not, however, constitute by themselves an "economic theory": the latter is given by the original behavior equations, describing the behavior of people by relations which may involve interdependence between endogenous variables: e.g., consumers' demand depends on income. Given the system of such behavior equations, the "reduced form" can be derived.

Lecture 17: CONTINUATION OF LECTURE 16

Two special cases deserve discussion.

First, what is the relation between our result (16.6), and the "circulation velocity" theory of money which says

(17.1) $Y = Mv$

(17.1) implies that $\partial Y/\partial G = 0$, that is, [by (16.7)]

(17.2) $\lambda_r = 0$

The "circulation velocity" theory of money thus neglects the effect of interest rate upon cash holding. If (17.2) is accepted then $\partial Y/\partial M$ becomes simply $1/\lambda_y$. And since (17.1) also means that the constant term (16.9) equals zero, we have $\lambda_o/\lambda_y = 0$ and therefore $\lambda_o = 0$. That is, the demand-for-cash equation (16.3) coincides with the reduced form (16.6), both being expressed by (17.1). The level of money income is fully determined by the money stock, via the (emasculated) demand-for-cash equation; it is entirely independent of interest rate r, and of the propensity of consumers and entrepreneurs to demand goods! Keynes' contribution was to draw attention to the propensities to consume and invest, and to relate demand for cash to interest rate.

From the extreme "anti-Keynesianism" of (17.1) we now proceed to a second case under consideration, to an hypothesis constituting a bit of "extreme Keynesianism." This consists in stating that demand for cash tends to become infinitely elastic with respect to interest rate, as the interest rate approaches lower levels. Such a demand-for-cash equation (16.3) is drawn in Graph 17:I. (Note that we use here the M,r-plane, and give two different levels of Y; while on Graph 16:I:B, the demand-for-cash equation was represented by the two positively sloped lines in the Y,r-plane, for two different levels of M.)

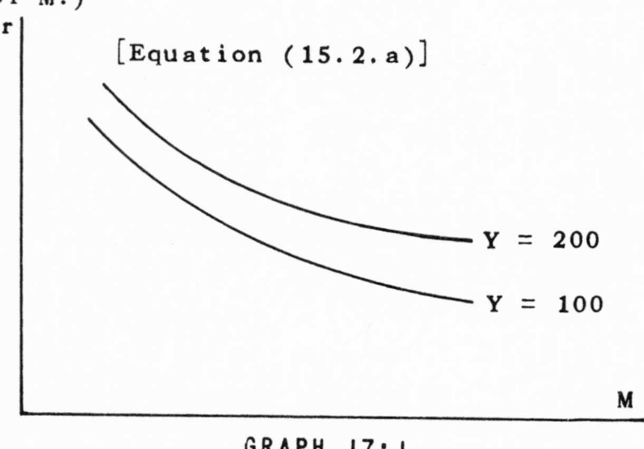

GRAPH 17:I

The asserted property is

$$(17.3)\quad \lambda_r \to \infty \text{ as } M \to \infty$$

$$(\text{i.e., } 1/\lambda_r \to 0 \text{ as } M \to \infty)$$

The asserted property, (17.3), is compatible with the general liquidity preference function (15.2.a) though of course not with the special linear case (15.2), in which λ_r is constant throughout. But since (16.8) is valid (for small changes) in any case, we see that (17.3) implies

$$(17.4)\quad \frac{\partial Y}{\partial M} \to 0 \text{ as } M \to \infty;$$

that is, monetary policy has a less strong effect upon money income as money stock reaches higher levels, and interest reaches lower levels. Hence money injection is neither useful (to overcome deflation) nor harmful (as a threat to price level in times of full employment), if interest rate is low. The assertion (17.3) from which this result is obtained was in turn derived from the theory that interest rate can never fall below a certain positive level since uncertainty about the future (including the possibility of rising interest rate) will always induce people to compete for cash (while the lenders will always charge a certain rate to cover handling costs).

The policy implication (17.4) was opposed around the end of War II by economists who rightly foresaw inflationary effects of the high money stock accumulated during the war. In this argument one should distinguish between two independent hypotheses:

(1) That (17.3) is false;

(2) That (16.1) should be reformulated to include money stock among the factors determining the demand for goods: Thus:

$$(17.5)\quad D = \delta_o - \delta_r r + \delta_y Y + \delta_M M,\ \delta_M > 0.$$ Compare with equation (3.1.a).

If (17.5) is accepted, then the "Keynesian" policy implication (17.4) becomes false even though the "Keynesian" assumption (17.3) (and the Graph 17:I) should be true. (The algebraic proof is left to students.)

Crudely, even if money stock should be unable to influence demand indirectly via interest rate (by cheapening the interest rate and thus inducing the businessmen to borrow for plant expansion) it is perhaps still able to influence demand directly. However, little is known about the size of the relevant coefficient δ_M in (17.5).

With demand for goods related to cash stock as in (17.5), our system has two relations involving cash stock and income:

(1) (17.5), describing the decision to demand goods, and especially

(in the case of consumers) the decision to consume rather than not to consume;

(2) (16.3), describing the decision to hold cash rather than securities.

The rationale of this behavior calls for closer microeconomic analysis.

Assumptions (17.3) and (17.5) have played a major role, not only in the recent discussions of inflation, but also in the discussion of wage policy. This will be taken up later.

* * * * * * * * * * *

PROBLEM 9

(Given as quarterly test at the end of the course.)

1. "The higher the national debt the higher the price level." Comment.

2. What are the conditions under which the relation between the quantity of money and the national money income, as derived from the equations expressing the behavior of consumers, businessmen and general cash-holders, would degenerate into the "equation of exchange"? (The "equation of exchange" says that national money income is proportional to the quantity of money.)

Lecture 18: "DEMAND CURVE FOR ALL GOODS"

Generalize our system, as given in the beginning of Lecture 16 in the following three directions simultaneously:

1) Buyers are affected not only by income and interest rate but also by cash stock M, as in (17.5).

2) Demand for goods is affected by disposable income $Y(1 - \tau)$ (where τ = tax rate) rather than by total income Y; or sti more generally: the demand for goods, and possibly also th demand for cash is affected by both Y and τ.

3) The functions involved are not necessarily linear; they will be denoted by Greek letters: δ, λ, ...; their partial derivatives will be denoted by Greek letters: δ_r, δ_y etc.

We have then:

$$D = \delta(r, Y, M, \tau),$$

$$(18) \quad D = Y - G$$

$$M = \lambda(r, Y, \tau).$$

It is understood that the following variables are exogenous: tax rate τ, government expenditure, G, and cash stock, M. The three equations then determine the three endogenous variables: total demand, D, (of consumers as well as businessmen) for goods, total income, Y, interest rate, r. Thus income, Y, (and also each of th other two endogenous variables) depends entirely on the following controlled conditions: τ, G, M; and on the following uncontrolled conditions: the behavior functions δ and λ. We shall express this by writing the "solution of the system":

$$Y = \phi(\tau, G, M; \delta, \lambda)$$

$$(18.a) \quad D = \psi(\tau, G, M; \delta, \lambda)$$

$$r = \chi(\tau, G, M; \delta, \lambda)$$

where the symbols "$= \phi(\ )$", etc., are equivalent to the words "depends on the quantities or functions listed in parentheses". A solution of a system of economic behavior relations--such as (18)-with respect to each of the endogenous variables, is also called th "reduced form of the system". It shows the effect of each of the conditions upon each of the endogenous variables. It is thus a guide to policies (compare also Lecture 1), provided something is known about the form and parameters of the functions (such as δ, λ involved.

The model (18) and consequently the reduced form (18.a) assume an unduly simplified form of government decision. This can be corrected to a certain extent, still retaining great simplicity in the system.

Instead of assuming G exogenous, we can take account of the fact that a part of the government expenditure--viz., the unemployment relief payments--depend on national income, for example

$$(18.1') \quad G = \gamma_0 + \gamma_1(Y_{max} - Y)$$

where Y_{max} is the national income at which no relief payments would be necessary, and γ_0 and γ_1 are certain policy constants depending on the government's previous commitments (such as war pensions) and on its past or current views as to the importance of unemployment relief and of other government goals. More generally, we can simply write

$$(18.1) \quad G = \gamma(Y),$$

where γ is a function (schedule) controlled by the government within known limits imposed by its previous commitments, the foreign situation, the constitution, etc. We have now one more endogenous variable, G; and one more equation, (18.1).

Similarly, the assumption that cash-stock, M, is arbitrarily fixed may be too unrealistic, even if (as in Lecture 15) we replace the statements

$$\left.\begin{array}{l} M = \lambda(r,Y), \\ M = \text{exogenous} \end{array}\right\}$$

by the statements

$$\left.\begin{array}{lll} \text{demand} & M^d & = \lambda(r, Y, \tau) \\ \text{supply} & M^s & = \text{exogenous} \\ \text{stock} & M & = M^d = M^s. \end{array}\right\}$$

It may be deemed more realistic to replace the statement on supply by a statement such as

$$(18.2) \quad M^s = \mu(r,Y),$$

where the function μ describes the policy (a schedule) which may be chosen by the banking authorities: they have decided that, at a given income level they will have a certain supply function, i.e., vary the volume of loans concomitantly with the interest rate in a certain way.

How do these amplified descriptions of the fiscal and monetary policy affect our reduced form (18.a)? Simply by replacing the quantities G, M (which now become endogenous) by the letters γ, μ which describe not quantities, but functions, viz., certain response patterns chosen by government and banking authorities. We have, then,

$$(18.b)\quad Y = \phi(\tau,\ \gamma,\ \mu;\ \delta,\ \lambda),$$

where the symbols after the semi-colon refer to the response patterns of the public, while those before the semi-colon give the response patterns of the government and are therefore at least partly controlled by the government.

We have thus summarized a model in which the demand for cash and for goods, the supply of cash and the supply of goods (national income) all enter the decisions of individuals and of public authorities as *sums of money*. We have denoted sums of money by capital Roman letters (see Lecture 2), reserving lower-case Roman letters for variables (such as the interest rate, r) which do not depend on the chosen unit of money*.) We have an identity (definitional relation), (2.2) or

$$(18.3)\quad y = Y/P,$$

so that (18.b) helps to relate *real income* to the various controlled and uncontrolled conditions as follows:

$$(18.4)\quad y = \phi(\tau,\ \gamma,\ \mu;\ \delta,\ \lambda)/P.$$

This can be represented by Graph such as 2:I, with the rectangular hyperbola ("demand curve for all goods") subjected to shifts which are caused, not necessarily by changes in money stock, M, but by changes in any or all of the controlled or uncontrolled conditions. Our new "demand curve for all goods" is a more general and sophisticated version of the old one, the equation of exchange (see also Lecture 17, first paragraph).

But now assume a different behavior on the part of both the private people and the government (including monetary) authorities: suppose they think entirely in terms of physical goods. Similar to the equation (3.1*), we have then to replace in our model the monetary terms (D, Y, G, M) by physical quantities (d, y, g, m); instead of (18) we have, say,

$$(18^*)\quad d = \delta^*(r,\ y,\ m,\ \tau),\ \text{etc.}$$

Obviously, the reduced form (18.a) or (18.b) will be replaced by one in which the real and not the money income is determined:

$$y = \phi(\tau,\ g,\ m;\ \delta^*,\ \lambda^*);\ \text{or more generally,}$$

$$(18.c)\quad y = \phi(\tau,\ \gamma^*,\ \mu^*;\ \delta^*,\ \lambda^*),$$

where γ^*, μ^* denote policy-schedules with regard to government spending and money supply. In (18.c) real income (quantity of physical goods supplied or level of production) is completely determined by

* We denote price level by P, measuring, as it were, the number of dollars per unit of an aggregate of physical goods. Alternatively one might regard the price level as the average of ratios between prices of various commodities in two years: a pure number, to be denoted by a lower-case letter.

fiscal and monetary policy, given people's response patterns. These latter response patterns (δ^*, λ^*) as well as the decisions of public authorities were assumed "free of money illusion", i.e., independent of any price changes that leave physical quantities unchanged (that is, are offset by proportional changes in money sums). No wonder that in (18.c) real income is shown to be independent of the price level. In the (P, y)-plane of Graph 2:I, the "demand curve for all goods" would be, in this case, represented by a *vertical line*, subjected to shifts that are due to changes in monetary or fiscal policies.

This extreme case of "freedom from money illusion" on the part of demanders for and suppliers of goods and cash is, of course, not realistic. At least the monetary authorities fix their policy in terms of dollars, and not of their physical ("deflated") equivalents. The governmental appropriations and the budgeting of firms' plans are, at least to a large part, fixed dollar-wise, although upward adjustments often follow a fast rise in prices. As to the consumers, who can say whether the housewife acts as in

$c = \alpha_1 y + \alpha_0$ ("no money illusion");

or as in

$C = \alpha_1 Y + \alpha_0$ ("money illusion", viz., "reckoning in dollars only"),

and hence

$c = \alpha_1 y + \alpha_0/P$;

or, thirdly, as in

$c = \alpha_1 y - \alpha_2 P + \alpha_0$ (another case of money illusion)?

Once "money illusion" is assumed on the part of at least one group of individuals, price level enters the system of behavior equations. Consequently (18.c) becomes

(18.5) $y = \phi(P;\ \tau,\ g,\ m;\ \delta,\ \lambda)$, or, more generally:

$$y = \phi(P;\ \tau,\ \gamma,\ \mu;\ \delta,\ \lambda).$$

Here the real income, an endogenous variable, is expressed as a function of exogenous variables (τ, g, m) and/or other controlled and uncontrolled conditions (Greek letters)*, and *in addition*, of the price-level, P, another endogenous variable. (18.4) is obviously a special case of (18.5). We have in (18.5) a "demand curve for all goods", but not necessarily in the form of the rectangular hyperbola.

(18.5)--or, for that matter, its special case, (18.4)--involves two

* We omit asterisks, as the function involved may or may not involve "money illusion".

endogenous variables, y and P. It is *not* a reduced form. It does not explain by itself how either y or P is determined by outside conditions. There must exist a further relationship between these same variables. We shall discuss this relationship--"the supply curve for all goods"--in the next lecture, to derive the effect of alternative policies upon y and P, as promised in the first lecture of this course.

Lecture 19: "SUPPLY CURVE FOR ALL GOODS" IN A FREE LABOR MARKET

Each of the relations (18.5) between real income (output) and price level was derived from behavior equations explaining the responses of people who demand goods or cash. With more brevity than profundity we shall call either of the equations (18.5) the "demand curve for all goods"; remembering, however, that it is not a behavior relation like (14.1) or (16.3). Rather, it is obtained by combining several behavior relations in an arbitrary way: viz., by eliminating endogenous variables except two (price and real income), whose relation can then be conveniently plotted on a plane under given controlled and uncontrolled conditions. Since we think of price and output as quantities fully determined by those conditions, there must exist a second relation between price and output, which we shall call, for brevity, "supply curve for all goods", and which we shall be able to plot on a plane. Again, this relation will be derived by combining certain behavior relations. We may regard those behavior equations as constituting the "supply sub-set" of the full system of behavior equations; and the equations treated in Lectures 3-18 as elements of the "demand sub-set".

Denote by n^d the aggregate demand of employers for labor, when the money wage rate W and the price level P are given. Denote by n^s the aggregate amount of labor which the individual workers are willing to offer at given W and P. Denote by n the actual level of employment. The following "supply sub-set" is worth considering:

(19.1) $n^d = \Delta(W, P)$: labor demand function

(19.2) $n^s = \sigma(W, P)$: labor supply function

(19.3), (19.4) $n = n^d = n^s$: determination of equilibrium employment in a free (i.e., non-unionized) labor market

(19.5) $y = \pi(n)$: short run production function, neglecting the output of the self-employed.

With the help of these 5 equations we can, in general, eliminate 5 out of the 6 variables involved (n, n^d. n^s, W, P, y). By eliminating all variables but P and y we obtain a "supply curve for all goods", under conditions of free labor market.

In the following example we shall assume more specially that employers' demand for labor is a decreasing function of the real wage rate only, while workers' supply of labor is an increasing function of the *money wage rate* only; finally, the output y increases with employment, but at a decreasing rate ("decreasing marginal returns to labor"). That is, remembering (19.3), (19.4), our "supply subset" of equations becomes:

	(19.a.1) $n = \Delta(W/P)$;	Δ a decreasing function
(19.a)	(19.a.2) $n = \sigma(W)$	; σ an increasing function
	(19.a.3) $y = \pi(n)$	; π a function that increases at decreasing rate.

On Graph 19.I, each of the equations (19.a.1), (19.a.2), is represented in the (n,P)-plane by a family of curves, each curve being drawn for one value of W. Thus when W = 1, employment = 60 million, and price level = 1. The locus of such intersection point shows how through the interplay of labor supply and labor demand, employment changes accompany changes of price level (whatever be the causes that make the price level change). On the right-hand side a scale for measuring the output $y = \pi(n)$ is indicated: output grows slower than employment.

On Graph 19.II, y is re-plotted on an ordinary scale: we obtain a "supply curve for all goods" which can now be shown together with a "demand curve for all goods" such as the curves of Graph 2:I which correspond to equation (18.4); or more generally, a curve representing (18.5). The position shift of the demand curve for all goods was shown in Lecture 18 to depend on certain controlled and uncontrolled conditions, viz., the fiscal and monetary policy and the behavior of those who demand cash or goods:

(19.6) $y = \varphi(P;\ \tau,\ \gamma,\ \mu,\ \delta,\ \lambda)$, say.

Similarly, the position of the supply curve for all goods depends on the conditions which figured in the "supply sub-set" (19.a); viz., on the behavior of those people who demand or supply labor, and on the production function:

(19.7) $y = \psi\ (P;\ \Delta,\ \sigma,\ \pi)$.

A change in any of the Greek variables, either in the demand curve, (19.6) or in the supply curve (19.7) leads to a change in the real income and/or price.

In (19.a) the demand for but not the supply of labor was assumed free of money illusion. As an extreme case, it was even assumed in (19.a.2) that workers are interested in money wage rates only and do not pay attention to prices. If, as another extreme, we assume workers interested in real wage rates only, then employment becomes independent of price-level, since the two equations

(19.b) $n = \Delta(W/P)$, $n = \sigma(W/P)$,

determine n and W/P. In this case, a change in price results in a proportional change of money wage-rate (and conversely), but does not affect employment. The SS-line of Graph 19:II becomes horizontal. Therefore no shift of the DD-line (i.e., no change in fiscal-monetary policy or in the propensity to consume, invest or hold cash) can affect real income and employment. This is sometimes de-

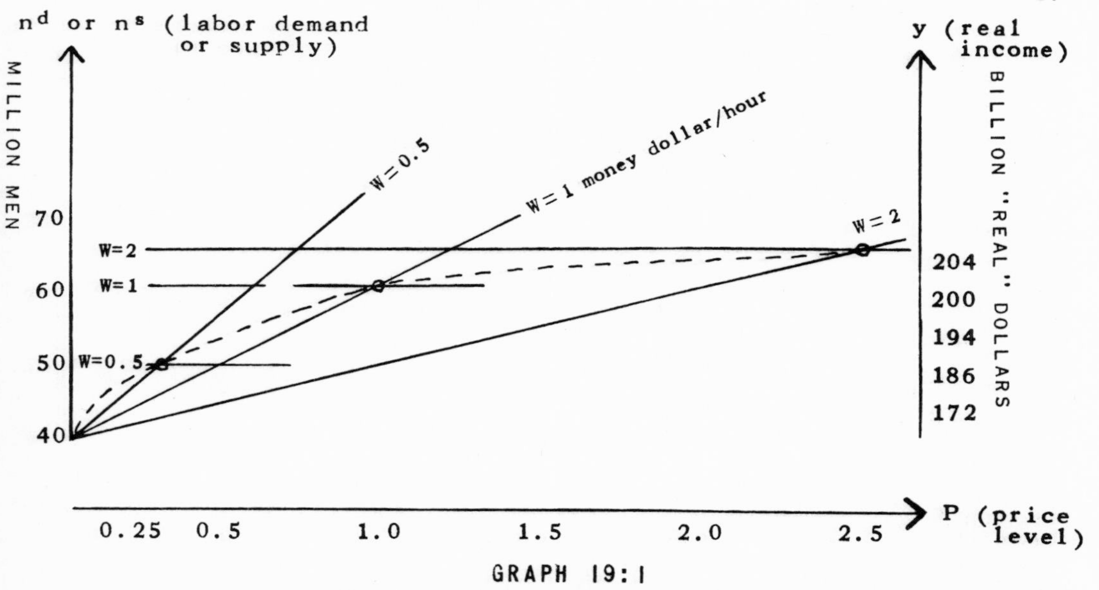

GRAPH 19:I

FREE LABOR MARKET: AN EXAMPLE

Sloping straight lines: labor demand function $n^d = 40 + 20P/W$

Horizontal lines: labor supply function $n^s = 70 - 10/W$

Circled points ⊙ ⊙ ⊙ satisfy $n^d = n^s$

Scale for y expresses a production function $y = \pi(n^d)$ such that marginal product = real wage offered by employers: $d\pi/dn^d = W/P = 20/(n^d - 40)$

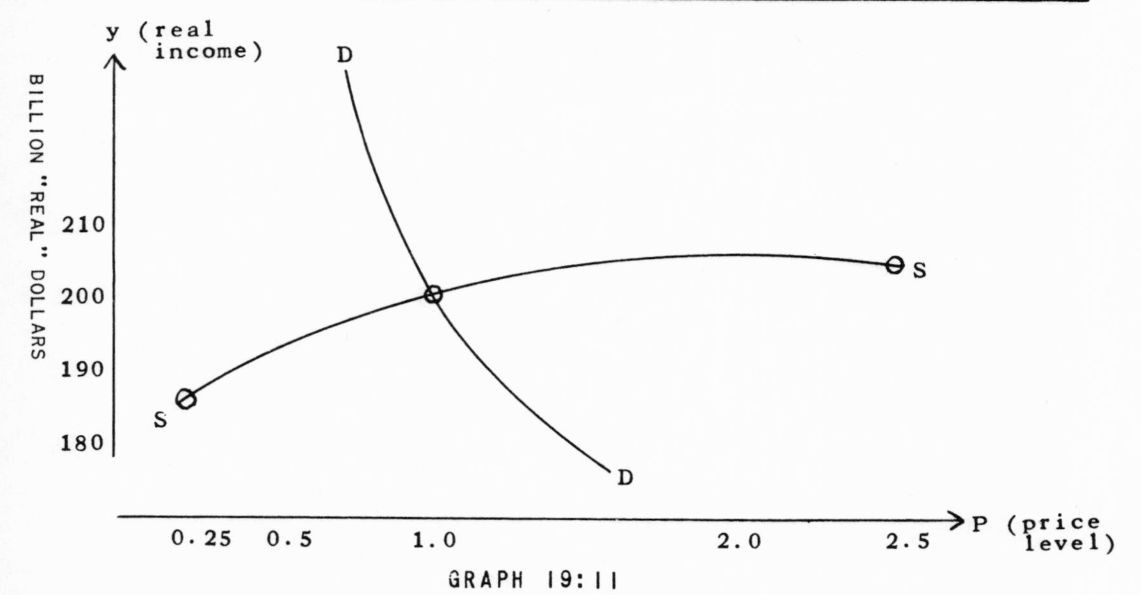

GRAPH 19:II

DETERMINATION OF PRICE & OUTPUT WHEN LABOR MARKET IS FREE

SS: supply curve for all goods, from Graph 19:I.

DD: demand curve for all goods, when money illusion is present in at least one equation of demand sub-set.

scribed as the "classical" or "anti-Keynesian" theory of the labor market.

On the other hand, to obtain an upward-sloping and not a horizontal SS-line, it is not necessary to make assumptions as narrow as (19.a Let us first maintain the assumption (19.a.1): labor demand is free from money illusion. But let us generalize (19.a.2) into $n^s = \sigma(W,P)$ thus:

(19.c)
(19.c.1) $n = \Delta(W/P)$, Δ a decreasing function
(19.c.2) $n = \sigma(W,P)$, σ an increasing function of W, and a decreasing function of P.

We still obtain the result that a price rise raises employment, provided the (positive) elasticity of σ with respect to W is numerically larger than its (negative) elasticity with respect to P. [Note that if the two elasticities were equal we would have again $n^s = \sigma(W/P)$, the "classical" case (19.b).] For example, suppose P is doubled. What will happen to W, and hence to W/P and to n? If W would also double, there would be an excess of labor supply (which we have assumed more elastic with respect to W than to P) over labor demand [which remains constant, by (19.c.1)]. If W would more than double, labor supply would be still larger, while the labor demand would fall; thus the excess of supply over demand would be even larger than if W had just doubled. Consequently, the equality of demand and supply in the labor market requires that a doubling of P is accompanied by less than doubling W; but then--by (19.c.1)--demand (and, consequently the supply) is increased. Thus (19.c) lead again to an upward-sloping supply curve (SS on Graph 19:II) for all goods, provided labor supply is more sensitive to changes in W than in P.

The maintaining of (19.c.1)--response of employers to real wages only--is, however, itself not necessary. It is usually derived from certain assumptions which can be partly relaxed. These conditions are:

(1) The only production factor considered is hired labor.
(2) Each firm maximizes its profit.
(3) Money wage-rates and prices are the same for each firm.

Condition (1) may be relaxed in two directions:

(a) An additional variable, capital, can be introduced into (19.a.1 and (19.a.3), to be defined in an additional (and dynamic) equation, "capital equals the sum of past investments". We shall not pursue this here since variations of aggregate capital over periods of a few years are, in fact, negligible in their effect upon output.

(b) The labor of the self-employed persons can be separated out, possibly as an exogenous variable; we shall refer to this fact in the next lecture.

Condition (2) helps to define the aggregate production function $y = \pi(n)$. This function, and also the aggregate marginal product $d\pi/dn$, is not defined, unless the distribution of labor between firms is known. If, in particular, condition (3) is replaced by the stronger statement that there is perfect competition between firms in buying labor and selling their product, then (2) implies

$$(19.8)\quad d\pi/dn^d = W/P,$$

as exemplified in the last line of the explanation to Graph 19:I. Under imperfect competition, however, (19.8) is, in general, invalid. But (2) and (3) still make each firm's labor demand, and hence the sum of these demands depend on W/P, as in (19.a.1); and still make the distribution of labor of firms, and hence the production function in (19.a.3), well determined.

For the purpose in hand it is, however, not necessary to maintain condition (2), profit-maximization. One may assume instead that each firm i (i = 1, 2, ...) has an individual demand function $n_i{}^d = \Delta_i(W,P)$, and an individual production function $y_i = \pi_i(n_i{}^d)$. Then, (with $n^d = n^s = n$)

$$(19.\text{d}.1)\quad n = \Delta_1(W,P) + \Delta_2(W,P) + \ldots = \Delta(W,P)$$

$$(19.\text{d})\qquad (19.\text{d}.2)\quad n = \sigma(W,P)$$

$$(19.\text{d}.3)\quad y = \pi_1[\Delta_1(W,P)] + \pi_2[\Delta_2(W,P)] + \ldots = \text{a function of } W,P \text{ [and hence, by (19.d.1), of } n\text{], that depends on } \Delta_1, \Delta_2 \ldots$$

Thus, in absence of profit maximization and perfect competition, the aggregate labor demand function is not related to the derivative (marginal product) of production function, and is not a function of real wage rate. The more general supply sub-set (19.d) still results in some "supply curve for all goods"--SS on Graph 19:II; whether this curve is upward sloping depends, of course, on the properties (e.g., elasticities with respect to W and P) of the generalized labor demand and supply functions. Assuming $\pi(n)$ always upward-sloping, a necessary and sufficient condition of SS to be upward-sloping is this: the elasticity of labor supply with respect to W must exceed its elasticity with respect to P in a larger proportion than the proportion by which the elasticity of labor demand with respect to W exceeds its elasticity with respect to P. This condition is likely to be fulfilled since, vaguely speaking, while both employers and workers are wage-conscious, the former are relatively more price-conscious than the latter. This is more general than the case studied earlier when the labor demand had equal elasticity with respect to wage and to price, while the wage-elasticity of labor supply was higher than its price-elasticity.

Thus, after dropping the assumptions of maximum profit and of perfect competition, we can still maintain Graph 19:II, and the pair of underlying "sub-sets" of equations, as an explanation of how the price level and the real income are determined in a free labor market, provided that hired labor is the only varying factor of production.

Lecture 20: DETERMINATION OF REAL INCOME AND PRICE LEVEL. TWO CONCEPTS OF INVOLUNTARY UNEMPLOYMENT

If there is no "money illusion" in any equation of the demand subset, the curve DD of Graph 19:II is horizontal: the "extreme Keynesian" case, implying the inability of wage-cuts to affect real income. If there is no "money illusion" in any equation of the supply subset, the curve SS of the same Graph is horizontal: the "classical" case, implying the inability of fiscal-monetary policy to affect real income. Let us inspect the "classical" case a little more closely, starting with a more general one.

On Graph 20:I:a, the labor market equations of Graph 19:I are replotted, using this time the horizontal axis to plot, not the price P, but the real wage-rate w = W/P. Since on Graph 19:I [as in equations (19.a)] labor demand but not labor supply was free of money illusion, the former is now represented, in the (w,n)-plane, by a single (downward sloping) curve, but the latter by a family of (upward sloping) curves, each corresponding to a different price level. We recognize the (circled) equilibrium points of Graph 19:I. (See next page for Graphs 20:I:a and b.)

If the still more general assumptions (19.d) were made, i.e., neither labor demand nor labor supply were free of money illusion, each would be represented by a family of curves, so that to each price-level would correspond a different pair of curves; we should again have a set of intersection points, one for each price level.

On the other hand, Graph 20:I:b represents the "classical" case, equations (19.b). In this case, at a given real wage rate neither the demand for nor the supply of labor is affected by price. Consequently each is represented by a unique curve and not by a family of curves. The intersection of these two curves gives the real wage rate and the employment level at which labor demand and labor supply balance.

Accordingly, in the "classical" case employment is independent of price. The supply curve (SS) for all goods is, in this case, not upward sloping as in the general case represented on Graph 20:II:a (which is a reproduction of Graph 19:II); instead, the SS-curve is horizontal, as on Graph 20:II:b. In this case, the price level only, but not the real income (and consequently not the employment level) can be influenced by shifts in the demand curve (DD) for all goods. (See Page 20:62 for Graphs 20:II:a, b and c.) Real income (and employment) can, in this case, be influenced only by shifts in the supply curve (SS). These shifts can originate, in this as in any other case, only in changes of the production function $\pi(n)$, the employers' demand schedule Δ, or the laborers' supply schedule σ. In particular, if the workers become willing to offer the same work at a lower wage-rate (or more work at the same wage-rate), i.e., if

GRAPHS 20:I:a and 20:I:b

FREE LABOR MARKET

No money illusion in labor demand.
Downward sloping line: labor demand function $n^d = 40 + 20/w$.
Circled points satisfy $n^d = n^s$.

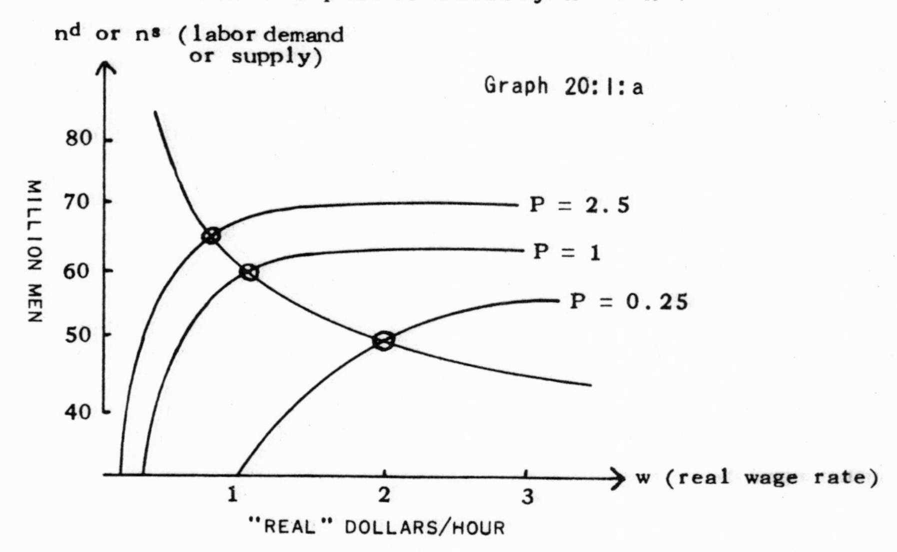

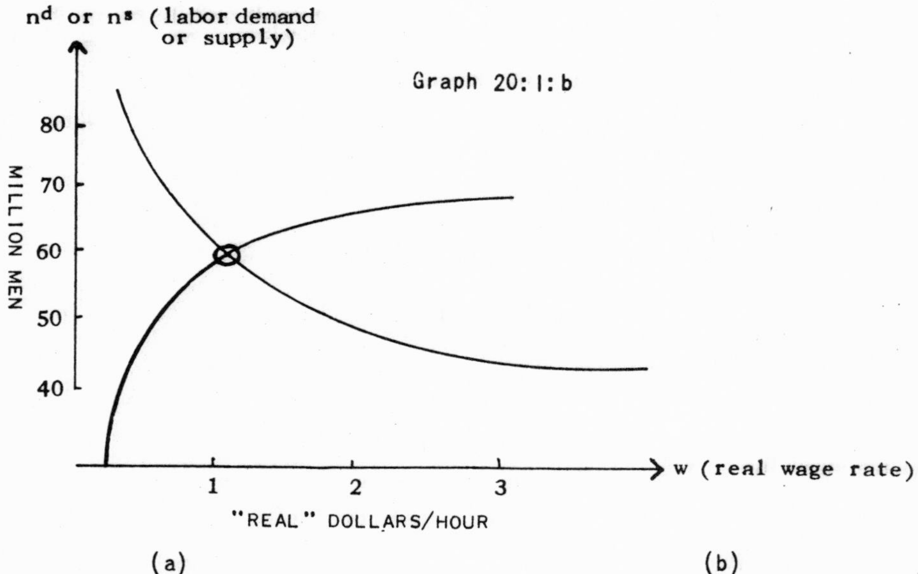

(a)

Money illusion in labor supply.
Upward sloping family: labor supply function $n^s = 70 - 10/wP$.
This Graph 20:I:a repeats Graph 19:I but is drawn in (w,n)-plane instead of (P,n)-plane.
Some points where $n^d = n^s = n$:
$n = 50$; $P = 0.25$; $w = 2$; $W = 0.5$.
$n = 60$; $P = 1$; $w = 1$; $W = 1$.
$n = 65$; $P = 2.5$; $w = 0.8$; $W = 2$.

(b)

No money illusion in labor supply.
Upward sloping line: labor supply function $n^s = 70 - 10/w$.

Unique point where $n^d = n^s = n$:

$n = 60$; $w = 1$;
W and P arbitrary.

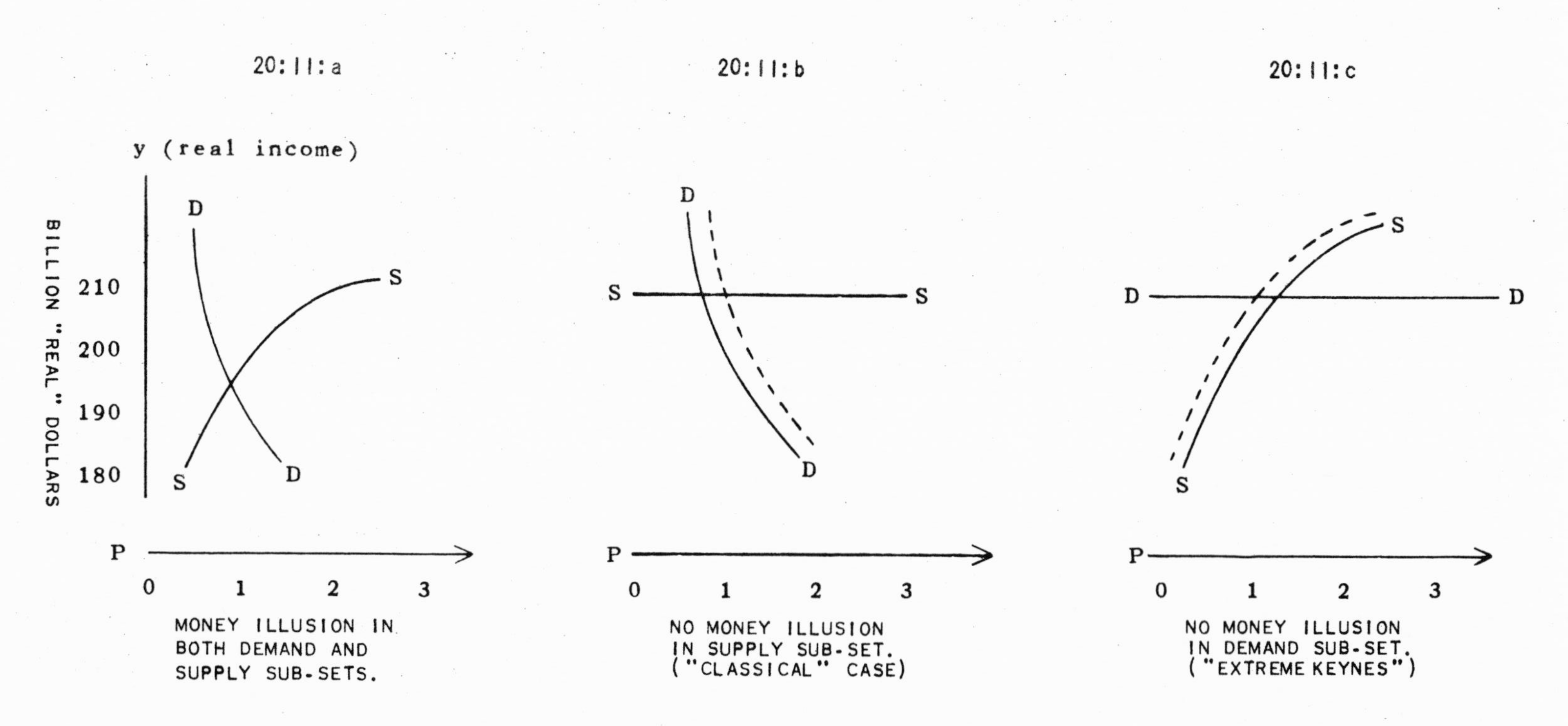
GRAPH 20:11:a, b, and c
DETERMINATION OF PRICE AND OUTPUT WHEN LABOR MARKET IS FREE
20:11:a
20:11:b
20:11:c
y (real income)
BILLION "REAL" DOLLARS
210
200
190
180
D
S
P
0
1
2
3
MONEY ILLUSION IN BOTH DEMAND AND SUPPLY SUB-SETS.
NO MONEY ILLUSION IN SUPPLY SUB-SET. ("CLASSICAL" CASE)
NO MONEY ILLUSION IN DEMAND SUB-SET. ("EXTREME KEYNES")

they revise their evaluation of leisure vs. goods, the labor supply curve on Graph 20:I:b will shift to the left; employment will increase while real wage-rate will fall. Thus, it is in the workers' power to increase employment; while monetary and fiscal policies--the shifting of DD-curve on Graph 20:II:b--cannot affect employment but can result only in changing the price level! All unemployment is voluntary.

The extreme opposite case occurs if, as on Graph 20:II:c, not the "supply curve (SS) for all goods", but the "demand curve (DD) for all goods" is horizontal. This would be the case if all decisions listed in the "demand sub-set" (Lecture 18)--private decisions as well as those of fiscal and monetary public authorities--were made in the absence of money illusion. In this case, real income and hence (via the production function) employment is completely determined by those decisions. The revision of workers' willingness to work, causing a shift in the SS-curve, would change price-level, but not employment. All unemployment is involuntary!

This result does not need the narrow assumption (19.c.1) (labor demand free of money illusion because employers maximize current profits). In this case, if real income and employment are determined by fiscal and monetary policy, the real wage rate is also determined, since to each level of employment corresponds only one real wage-rate (equal to the marginal product of labor). But this ceases to be necessarily true under the more general assumption (19.d.1), where n^d is some function of W and P, not necessarily of their quotient W/P. Furthermore, the existence of self-employed labor, not subjected to the money wage cuts hitting hired employees, also prevents prices from following the money wage rates exactly, even if the demand for labor were a function of real wage rate. (To prove this, use n to denote the hired, and n' the self-employed labor; denote their money rewards per hour by W and W' respectively, and study the effect of changing W when W' remains constant).

The assumption that the "demand sub-set" but not the "supply sub-set" is free of money illusion leads thus, under conditions of a free labor market, to the proposition that a revision of workers' supply schedule (σ) can lead to no change in employment but only to a change in prices (not necessarily proportional to the money wage cut).

This concept of involuntary unemployment has been used in particular by A. P. Lerner in his various writings on Keynesian theory (partly summarized in his "Economics of Control"). It is in line with Book V of Keynes' "General Theory". However, there also exists quite a different concept of involuntary unemployment: the excess of the labor supply n^s (number of people willing to work at a given W and P) over employment n. The equations--used by us so far--of a quickly adjusted free labor market

$$(19.4),\ (19.3)\quad n = n^d = n^s$$

are, of course, not compatible with the phenomenon of involuntary unemployment thus defined. It presupposes a different view of the labor market. As in other markets where the equalization of a demand and supply is slowed up or obstructed by technological or institutional causes (e.g., the housing market), we may have to replace the two equations (19.4), (19.3) by a single equation

(20.1) $n = \text{Min}(n^d, n^s)$:

employment is equal to either the demand for or the supply of labor, whichever is smaller. It is understood that n^d and n^s are derived as before by aggregating the labor demand schedules of individual employers and the labor supply schedules of individual workers, respectively. In the resulting equations

$n^d = \Delta(W,P)$; $n^s = \sigma(W,P)$,

the symbols Δ, σ have the same meaning as in Lecture 19. Equation (20.1) says that if $n^d > n^s$, then employers cannot press into the workshops more workers than those willing to work at existing W and P; and if $n^s > n^d$, the workers willing to work at existing W and P but not offered jobs cannot force themselves upon the employers. This is a fair description of our institutions. If $n^s < n^d$, the difference $n^d - n^s$ is called labor shortage. This more or less on the lines of Keynes' Book I, where willingness (of individuals) to work at existing wages and prices is emphasized; though it was probably not too clear to Keynes that this concept is really different from that of Book V; nor is it made clear (p. 15) that when n is exceeded by n^s, n is not also exceeded by n^d but is equal to it [equation (20.1)]. "Involuntary unemployment" *in the first sense* (inability of wage-cuts to raise employment) is clearly not involuntary in the sense that not all people willing to work at existing W and P get jobs. They *all do*. If $n = n^d = n^s$, then the number of actually filled jobs, n, $= \sigma(W,P) =$ the number of jobs wanted at the existing money wage rate W and existing price level P.

With the single equation (20.1) replacing the two equations $n = n^d = n^s$, one equation is lacking to make the system determinate. The failure of labor demand and supply quickly to become equal to each other is explained by the fact that the wage-bargaining is done by unions rather than by individuals. The action of the unions (or of the joint bargaining bodies, possibly including a public arbiter or the government) must be expressed by an equation of the system. As the simplest postulate we may write

(20.2) $W = \overline{W}$

where $\overline{W}$ is an exogenous quantity fixed independently of current economic variables; or, possibly more realistically,

(20.2.a) $W = \Omega(n,P)$,

indicating that the outcome of bargaining depends on employment (or real income) and price level. One might be tempted to call (20.2.a)

--if rewritten with n on the left hand side--a "labor supply function of the unions". But this expression would be confusing and would wrongly depict the union decision as that of labor contractors delivering varying quantities of men (or man-hours) depending on varying wage offers.

Graph 20:III uses for simplicity the special labor demand and labor supply functions of Graph 19:I: individual firms react to real wage rates, while individual workers react to money wage rates only (and not to W *and* P, which would be a more general case of money illusion). But since the labor market is now considered unionized, the condition $n^d = n^s = n$ is dropped, and union action introduced, thus:

$$\begin{aligned} n^d &= \Delta(W/P) \\ n^s &= \sigma(W) \\ n &= \mathrm{Min}(n^d,\ n^s) \\ W &= \overline{W}. \end{aligned} \qquad (20.3)$$

Graph 20:III is obtained accordingly from Graph 19:I by erasing, for each level of W, that part of the labor demand curve where demand exceeds supply; and that part of the labor supply curve where supply exceeds demand. The remaining segments constitute, for each level of W, a relation between employment n and price P: a /‾-shaped line, one for each value of $W = \overline{W}$ fixed by the unions. To the left of the "kink" there is involuntary unemployment; to the right, labor shortage.

Using now the production function $y = \pi(n)$--the same as on Graph 19:I, right-hand scale--we can draw "supply curves for all goods" corresponding to the employment-price relations that were derived on Graph 20:III. We thus obtain Graph 20:IV. (See next page for Graphs 20:III and IV.) Each "supply curve for all goods" corresponds to a certain union-fixed money wage rate $\overline{W}$. The "demand curve (DD) for all goods" is thus intersected in different points, depending on $\overline{W}$. Union action is responsible for the shifts of the "supply curve for all goods"; monetary and fiscal policy is (as before) responsible for shifts (not shown on the graph) of the "demand curve for all goods", DD.

Should DD be horizontal (due to absence of money illusion throughout the demand sub-set of the system), the situation already discussed for the case of the free labor market would repeat itself in the present case of the unionized labor market. No action of the unions can affect real income and employment if real income is completely determined by other factors outside of the unions' control. In such a case, we would have, in general, involuntary unemployment in both senses: in the sense of ineffectiveness of wage-cuts as well as in the sense that some unemployed people are willing to work at the current wage rate and price level.

It would be desirable to replace assumptions (20.3) by more general ones:

GRAPH 20:III

UNIONIZED LABOR MARKET (USING LABOR DEMAND AND SUPPLY FUNCTIONS OF GRAPH 19:I)

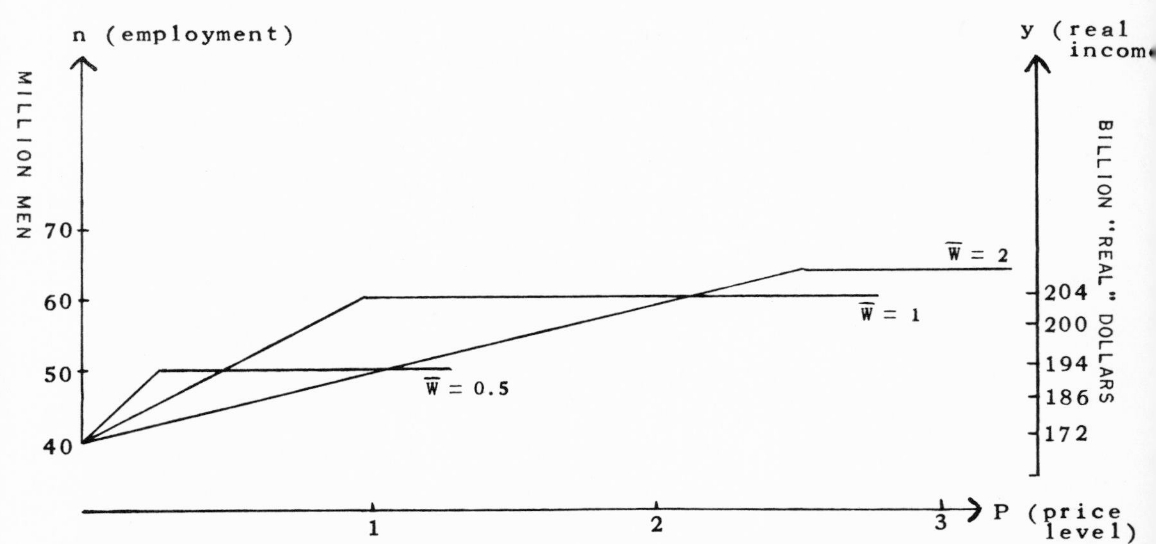

GRAPH 20:IV

DETERMINATION OF PRICE AND OUTPUT WHEN LABOR MARKET IS UNIONIZED.

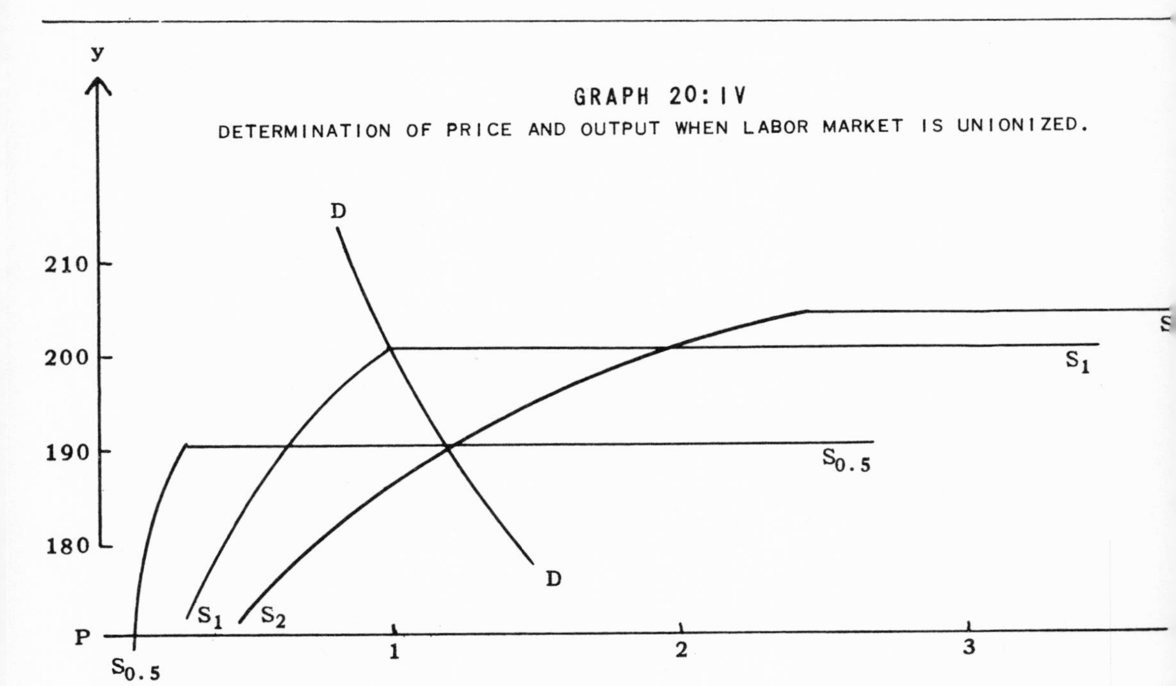

DD: demand curve for all goods (not free of money illusion). SS (viz., S_1S_1, S_2S_2, ... when W = 1, 2, ...): supply curves for all goods, depending on union-fixed money wage rate W and derived from Graph 20:III.

1) the labor demand and supply functions should be generalized into $\Delta(W,P)$ and $\sigma(W,P)$, as in (19.d):

2) the union action should be expressed, not by (20.2), but by the more complicated assumption (20.2.a), which does not regard unions as completely independent of economic conditions. The fact that union bargaining is to a certain extent influenced by government policy can be taken care of by varying the function Ω (the unions' "schedule" of action).

We must conclude here by reminding ourselves of the program set out in Lecture 1: to evaluate the effect of alternative conditions upon employment n and price level P. The controlled conditions (policies) considered were τ, μ (or $\overline{M}$), γ (or $\overline{G}$)--as discussed in Lecture 17; we have now added to them Ω (or $\overline{W}$). The uncontrolled conditions are the functions δ, λ of Lecture 17; and the functions Δ, σ, π of Lecture 18. Graphs such as 20:II (the case of the free labor market) or 20:IV (for the case of the unionized labor market) summarize the system by conveniently splitting it into a "demand sub-set" and a "supply sub-set", resulting respectively in the demand and the supply curve "for all goods." The "extreme Keynesian" and the "classical" cases, in which one of the two curves is horizontal, arise when either the demand sub-set or the supply sub-set of equations is free of "money illusion", i.e., if the corresponding decisions run in real terms only. These extreme cases deserve attention because of their policy implications, already listed in Table 1:I. According to whether actual facts are nearer the one or the other extreme hypothesis, more stress has to be laid on fiscal-monetary, or on money wage-rate policy.*

---

* NOTE: Examine also Problem 10 below, used as a test at the end of the quarter. This problem involves a policy of fixing *real* wage rates, as attempted recently in the contract between General Motors and the United Automobile Workers.

PROBLEM 10

(Given as quarterly test at the end of the course.)

ASSUME:

Number of physically employable persons = 65 million;
Money income constant at $180 billion;
Demand for labor (in millions) = n^d = $-2w + 62$, where
w = real wage rate in "1950 dollars" per hour.
Supply of labor (in millions)
$n^s = (1/2)(wp) + 60$; where p = price level (1950 = 1);
Employment = $n = n^d$ (neglect the possible case of labor shortage).
Real wage rate fixed by unions from time to time;
Net real output in "1950 dollars" = 3000 n;

QUESTION: What is the effect of raising the real wage rate from 1 to 2 "1950 dollars" per hour, upon:

1) "objective" unemployment, i.e., difference between

the number of physically employable people and the employment;

2) price level;

3) "involuntary" unemployment defined as the difference between the number of people willing to work and the employment.

* * *

ANSWER:

When $w = 1$ and $p = 1$, then $n = n^d = -2 + 62 = 60$

$n^s = 1/2 + 60 = 60\ 1/2$

Objective unemployment $= 65 - 60 = 5$

Involuntary " $= 60\ 1/2 - 60 = 1/2$

When $w = 2$, then $n^d = -4 + 62 = 58$;

Objective unemployment $= 65 - 58 = 7$

Real income $= y = 3n = 174$

$p = 180/174 = 1.034$

$n^s = (1/2)(2)(180/174) + 60 = 61.034$

Involuntary unemployment $= 61.034 - 58 = 3.034$

SUMMARY:

	$w = 1$	$w = 2$
	$p = 1$	$p = 1.034$
$n^d - n_{max}$	$= 5$	$= 7$
$n^s - n^d$	$= 0.5$	$= 3.034$

SUPPLEMENTARY LECTURE I

NOTE: Lectures 1-20 were given in 1948. Notes of those lectures were also distributed as reading material to the class of 1949. In 1949, Supplementary Lectures I-III were given as an introduction and were followed by the discussion of Problems 11-81.

(See also Lecture 1.)

The result of a man's action depends on: a) this action; and on b) conditions beyond his control. Action is also called "policy", or "controlled conditions". Action is called rational if it leads to the best result achievable under given uncontrolled conditions.

Example: Suppose that real national income depends on: a) taxes and loans of the government; and on b) the people's consumption habits and technical skills; and suppose the government regards a high real national income as preferable to a low one. A rational government would choose tax and loan policies that would achieve the highest real national income that can be achieved at given habits and skills of the people. To make this choice it is necessary to know in what way the national income depends upon taxes, government loans, habits and skills.

More generally, the government's targets may include, besides the real income of the nation, some other variables such as "lack of involuntary unemployment", "price stability: neither inflation nor deflation", etc. As to the means at the government's disposal, they may include monetary besides fiscal policy. Moreover, although the fixation of wage rates is not a constitutional prerogative of the U.S. government, we shall treat wage policy on the same footing as monetary and fiscal policy, for two reasons: a) the government plays a growing role as a wage arbitrator; b) the economist is called to advise the "public opinion", the "people", on what would be the results of a given action of the collective bargaining agencies; it being presumed that the "people" can influence not only the officers of constitutional government, (e.g., by giving or withdrawing votes) but also the officers of bodies such as the labor unions (e.g., by affecting the votes of individual union members) or the business corporations. The term "public policy" includes wage policy along with monetary and fiscal policy, with the "people" as the decision-making agent. Alternatively, one may agree to use the term "government policy" in a wide, *de facto* sense. Policy is always defined with reference to some decision-making agent and is assumed to be under this agent's full control.

To choose the best policy it is necessary to know how the relevant targets are affected by both controlled and uncontrolled conditions. It would be possible to find this in a purely empirical way if economic history recorded a sufficient number and variety of situations --e.g., if many possible tax and wage levels under many possible psychological, technological and weather conditions had been observed in the past; or if such situations could be produced, one after another, by experiment. In both cases, one would find the effect of, say, taxes and weather upon employment by using the "multiple regression" (also called "least squares") statistical method; this would also allow for the effect of non-measurable and non-specifiable random influences, of great importance in the social field.

However, historically recorded situations are not numerous and not varied enough; and experiments are seldom possible. The economist draws on an additional source of information: he knows something about the plausible behavior of individual men when they respond to changes in their conditions. These conditions include not only the controlled and uncontrolled conditions defined above--such as taxes and weather; but also a third set of variables which we shall call "economic" (or "endogenous") variables: for example, the individual's income, or (in absence of price control) the level of prices. The way in which the individuals respond (their "psychology", or "habits") is itself, from the point of view of the government, a "non-controlled condition", similar to weather. So-called economic theory is based on listing plausible response patterns of individuals, patterns that are compatible with the economist's general experience of the behavior of men, including himself. This experience includes in particular the observation that, on the whole, people's behavior, at least in matters of material well-being, is not too far from "rational" behavior described at the beginning of this lecture. This leads to the principle of "maximizing profits" and more generally, "maximizing utility", from which much (but not all) of economic theory is derived.

SUPPLEMENTARY LECTURE II

(See also Lecture 20, in particular pp. 20.64 seq.)

To exemplify the ideas of Lecture I consider the following description of a hypothetical society: PROPOSITION 1. Workers are willing to work more if money wage rate is increased. PROPOSITION 2. Employers are willing to hire more workers if money wage rate is decreased, or price level increased. PROPOSITION 3. Employers cannot employ more labor than workers offer; nor can workers get more jobs than employers offer; and employment cannot be, at the same time, smaller than both the supply of labor and the demand for it. PROPOSITION 4. Money wage rate is fixed politically. PROPOSITION 5. Price level is fixed politically.

We shall denote by capital Latin letters the quantities that depend, and by lower case Latin letters the quantities that do not depend, on the choice of the money unit. Thus W = money wage rate, P = price, $w = W/P$ = real wage rate. Write: n^d = demand for labor, n^s = supply of labor, n = employment, all in man-years per year. The levels at which a variable is fixed politically will be denoted by a bar, thus: $\overline{W}$, $\overline{P}$. Greek letters will denote functional relations ("schedules") between two or more variables. The five propositions are then restated thus:

(II.1) $n^s = \sigma(W)$; $d\sigma/dW > 0$ (read: derivative of σ with respect to W is positive).

(II.2) $n^d = \delta(W,P)$; $\partial\delta/\partial W < 0$, $\partial\delta/\partial P > 0$ (read: partial derivatives of δ with respect to W and to P, respectively, negative and positive).

(II.3) $n = \mathrm{Min}(n^s, n^d)$ (read: n equals n^s or n^d, whichever is smaller).

(II.4) $W = \overline{W}$

(II.5) $P = \overline{P}$

Equations (II.1), (II.2) are behavior equations. The "labor supply function" (or "schedule") σ is "given psychologically" inasmuch as it depends on the workers' "taste", their "preference scale" (viz., their choice between leisure and money). The "labor demand function" δ is "given psychologically" inasmuch as it depends on the employers' hopes and fears regarding the future market for their product, and on their keenness in trying to find that production level at which the expected profit will be maximized; but δ also depends on "technology" (production function, to be introduced in a later, more complete system) and on the degree of monopoly in the product and labor markets, a "sociological" datum. (See also Lecture 19, p. 19.59).

Equation (II.3) can be called an "institutional" one: it would become invalid if slavery were introduced or if workers "occupied the factories" (as in Italy 1920).

Equations (II.4), (II.5) are also "institutional": They state the existence of wage control and price control.

To fix the ideas by an example let us specify the functions σ and δ numerically as follows:

$$(II.1') \quad n^s = 70 - 10/W$$

$$(II.2') \quad n^d = 40 + 20\,P/W,$$

where n^s, n^d are measured in million man-years, W is measured in dollars per man hour, and P is a price index. The resulting levels for n^d, n^s, n, and also for the difference $n^d - n^s$ (labor shortage, if positive; involuntary unemployment, if negative) are given below, for a few selected levels of W and P: Chart II.1.

CHART II.1

LABOR SUPPLY, DEMAND, EMPLOYMENT, AND SHORTAGE
FOR SELECTED LEVELS OF CONTROLLED MONEY WAGE RATE AND PRICE
WHEN EQUATIONS (II.1'), (II.2'), (II.3) ARE VALID.

W	n^s	n^d		P = .5	P = 1	P = 1.25
.5	50	40 + 40 P	n^d =	60	80	90
			n =	50	50	50
			$n^d - n^s$ =	10	30	40
1.0	60	40 + 20 P	n^d =	50	60	65
			n =	50	60	60
			$n^d - n^s$ =	−10	0	5
2.0	65	40 + 10P	n^d =	45	50	52.5
			n =	45	50	52.5
			$n^d - n^s$ =	−20	−15	−12.5

For a more comprehensive presentation, plot equations (II.1') and (II.2') on a diagram, with P and n^d (also n^s, n) as the axes: see the solid lines of Graph 19.I, Lecture 19, p. 19.57). Then, with the help of (II.3) one obtains, for any given level of W, a relation between employment n and price level P (see Graph 20:III), represented by a broken line. On Chart II.2 below, we show this relation when W = 1, and hence when $n^s = 60$, $n^d = 40 + 20$ P. (Turn to next page for Chart II.2).

CHART II.2

RELATION BETWEEN EMPLOYMENT AND CONTROLLED PRICE LEVEL WHEN MONEY WAGE RATE IS FIXED ($W = 1$) AND EQUATIONS (II.1'), (II.2'), (II.3) ARE VALID

$\sigma\sigma$ = labor supply curve
$\delta\delta$ = labor demand curve

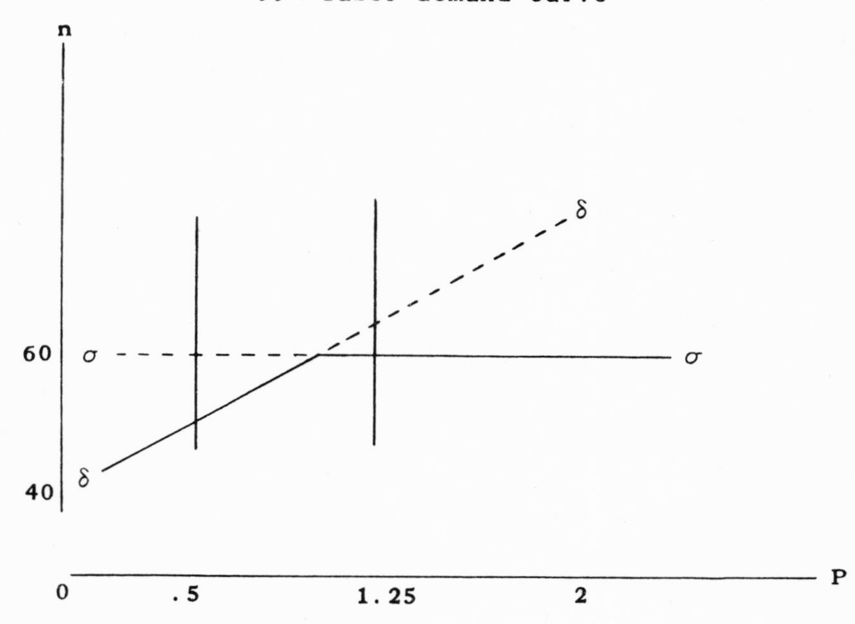

The dotted line-segments indicate the "ineffective" parts of the labor-supply and labor-demand functions. Note that when price level = .5 (and W = 1), there is "involuntary unemployment", $n^s - n^d = 10$; when P = 1.25 (and W = 1, as before), there is "labor shortage" $n^d - n^s = 5$; but when P = 1 (and still W = 1) labor demand and labor supply are equal. We have used the wage-control equation (II.4) by fixing $\bar{W} = 1$; according to the price control equation (II .5), price is also fixed, as indicated by each of the vertical lines.

The following result is important: an increase of the fixed price has no effect on employment (and merely increases labor shortage), if the fixed price exceeds already the level at which demand equals supply, viz., P = 1; but as long as this level is not reached, the increase in the fixed price (the wage rate always assumed fixed) does result in higher employment. Note also that this critical level would be a different one (viz., higher) if the wage-rate were fixed not at W = 1 but at a higher level: (see position of the "kinks" on Graph 20:III).

To study similarly the way in which employment is influenced by a changing wage rate (the price level being fixed), it is convenient to re-plot equations (II.1'), (II.2'), now with W instead of P as the horizontal axis: Chart II.3 on next page.

CHART II.3

RELATION BETWEEN EMPLOYMENT AND CONTROLLED MONEY WAGE RATE WHEN PRICE LEVEL IS FIXED (P = 1) AND EQUATIONS (II.1'), (II.2'), (II.3) ARE VALID

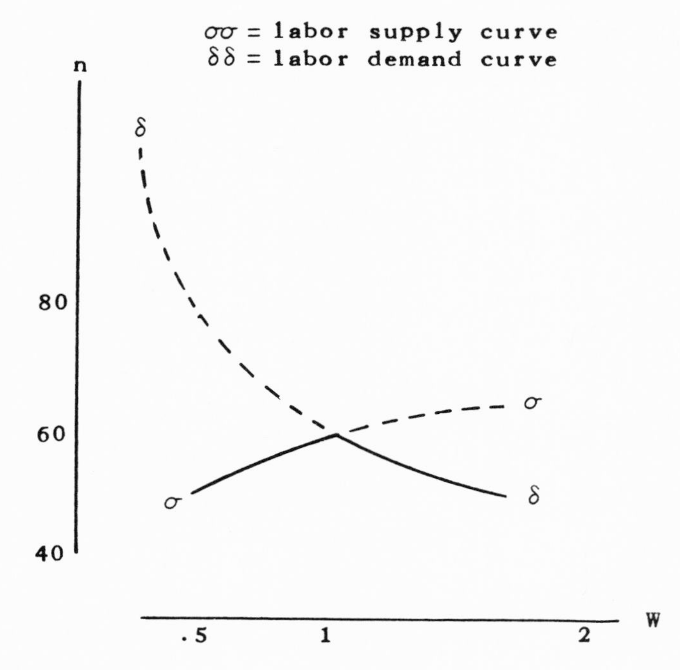

Again, the dotted line segments indicate the "ineffective" parts of the labor demand and labor supply functions. Note that there is an "optimal" money wage-rate (W = 1), at which employment reaches its peak and demand and supply are equalized; if money wage rate deviates from this position, either upward or downward, employment falls. Note that this position itself depends on the price level: if P were increased, the (downward sloping) demand curve would shift upwards, while the (upward sloping) supply curve would remain unmoved; the abscissa of the intersection point, i.e., the optimal money wage rate would increase.

After the arithmetic of our first Chart, and the geometry of the other two, look at our system of equations (II.1) to (II.5) algebraically. These five equations can be solved for the five "economic variables"

n^s, n^d, n, W, P.

Thus employment n will depend on the quantities $\overline{W}$, $\overline{P}$, and the functions σ, δ, and on nothing else. Write

(II.A) $n = \phi(\overline{P}, \overline{W}, \sigma, \delta)$;

we shall always use ϕ to mean "depends on the quantities and functions listed in the parentheses and on nothing else". Suppose high employment is to be combined with the absence of labor shortage as well as of involuntary unemployment. That is, suppose these are targets in the sense of Lecture I. Then the policy-deciding agent will choose $\overline{P}$ and $\overline{W}$ such as to make n a maximum, and at the same time make $n^d = n^s$, given the uncontrolled conditions σ, δ. It happens that the particular equations (II.1'), (II.2') used for our example, will not give a finite solution for $\overline{W}$: see Chart II.3 and raise the price level thus shifting $\delta\delta$ upward; but if an upper limit is put upon either n or $\overline{W}$, the problem becomes soluble.

Suppose now there is no price control. Proposition 5 and equation (II.5) disappear. The remaining 4 equations do not suffice to determine n as a single number. But they do suffice to determine a schedule, a relationship between n and P, such as drawn (for W = 1) on Chart II.2. This curve will shift only if at least one of the givens ($\overline{W}$, σ, δ) changes. We write now, instead of (II.A),

$$\text{(II.B)} \quad n = \phi(P; \overline{W}, \sigma, \delta).$$

In (II.A), the parentheses contained givens only. In (II.B), a semicolon separates a variable, P, from the givens $\overline{W}$, σ, δ. Equation (II.B) says that we are interested in the relation between n and P, and that this relation itself depends on $\overline{W}$, σ, δ (and on nothing else).

In (II.B), the system (II.1) - (II.4) is reduced to one equation in two variables; to explain how n and P are determined we need another such equation: just like we need, in the market of a commodity, a supply and a demand equation, two relations between quantity and price. The missing relation takes the place of the dropped assumption of price control, (II.5).

A familiar example of thus completing our system in the absence of price control is the "quantity theory of money". Replace Proposition 5 by the following three:

PROPOSITION 5: money income is proportional to money stock. PROPOSITION 6: money stock is frozen politically. PROPOSITION 7: real income is the higher, the higher is employment. Or denoting national real income (measured in prices of that year in which P = 1) by y and, consequently, money income by Py:

$$\text{(II.5')} \quad Py = Mv;$$

$$\text{(II.6)} \quad M = \overline{M};$$

$$\text{(II.7)} \quad y = \pi(n), \ \partial\pi/\partial n > 0.$$

Here v is a behavior constant, called velocity of circulation. (Whether such a constant exists need not be discussed yet.) $\pi(n)$ is a "production function", in which factors other than labor are neglected; it expresses the state of technology. From (II.5') and (II.6), we obtain a relation

$$\text{(II.C)} \quad y = \overline{M}v/P.$$

(II.C) is plotted on Chart II.4, (for Mv = 125 billion dollars a year) as a downward sloping curve DD (a "rectangular hyperbola", a "curve with unit-elasticity", a "constant outlay curve"). (II.C) is sometimes called "demand function for the output as a whole"-- not too good a term.

CHART II.4

RELATION BETWEEN REAL INCOME (y) AND PRICE LEVEL WHEN MONEY WAGE RATE, MONEY STOCK, AND VELOCITY OF CIRCULATION ARE FIXED ($W = 1$, $Mv = 125$) AND EQUATIONS (II.1'), (II.2'), (II.3), (II.5'), (II.7) ARE VALID.

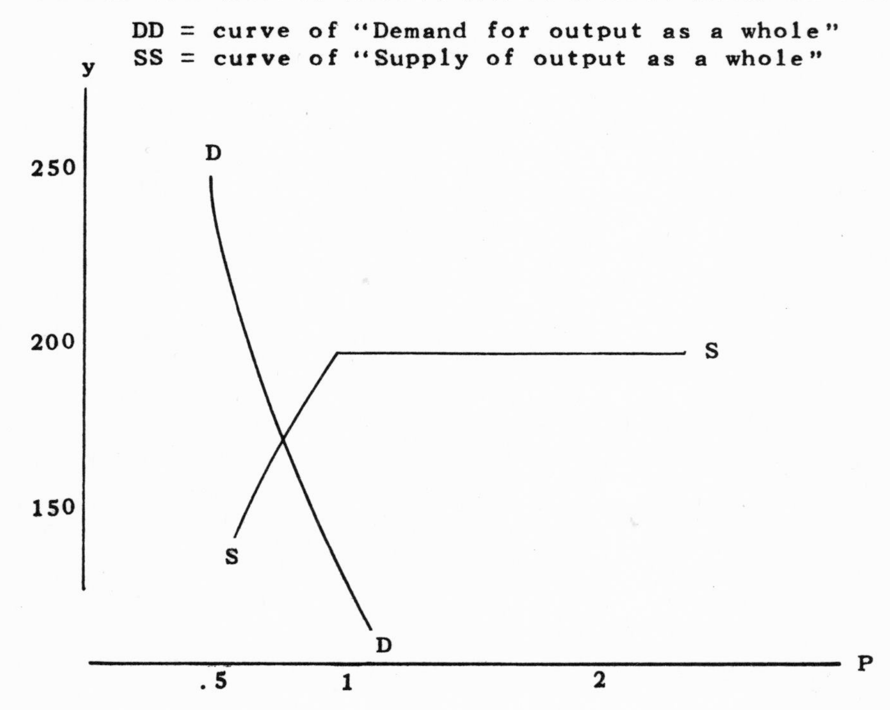

As to the production function (II.7), we can combine it with the equations (II.1)-(II.4) which had resulted in the supply curve for labor, (II.B). The latter was plotted, for $\overline{W}$ = \$ 1. -, on Chart II.2. Combining now (II.B) with the production equation (II.7) we translate labor supply into supply of commodities, i.e., obtain a relation between output y and price level P. This new relation depends on the same givens as (II.B) and, in addition, on the production function π:

$$\text{(II.D)} \quad y = \phi(P;\ \overline{W},\ \sigma,\ \delta,\ \pi).$$

It is plotted, on Chart II.4, for $\overline{W}$ = \$ 1. -, as the curve SS. It may be called "supply function for the output as a whole", but the term is not too good. Unlike a supply function for a single commodity, (II.D) does not describe the behavior of the sellers of this commodity; it is rather the result of interaction between the entrepreneurs and the workers. We can now solve (II.C), (II.D) for the two variables y, P. The solution, i.e., the pair of values of y, P that is consistent with the assumed equations is shown by the point of intersection on Chart II.4. Once y, P are thus determined, the solution values of n, n^d, n^s are also obtained. Each solution value will depend on some or all of the givens, viz.: $\overline{M}$, v, $\overline{W}$, σ, δ, and π.

In particular, an increase in M would shift the DD-curve upwards, and thus raise the price level P; *this shift would also raise the real income* y *(an important result!)*, provided the price was not already above a certain critical level (= 1 on our Chart, where W was fixed at $ 1.-).

We have treated a set of seven equations by grouping them into a "demand sub-set" consisting of (II.5'), (II.6), and a "supply sub-set" consisting of the other five, (II.1), (II.2), (II.3), (II.4), (II.7). Each of the two sub-sets was then reduced to one equation in the same pair of variables (y, P). This permitted an easy use of graphs but was not the only possible way of solving the system. For example, we might regard (II.5'), (II.6), (II.7) as one of two sub-sets and obtain from it the "missing relation" mentioned on p. II.75, para. 3:

$$\text{(II.E)} \quad n = \phi(P;\ \overline{M},\ v,\ \pi),$$

which together with (II.B) would give a determinate system. (II.E) could be plotted on the same graph with (II.B), viz., on Chart II.2.

A necessary (though not sufficient) requirement for an economic hypothesis, or theory (a system of relation between variables), is that it should lead to a determinate solution. If it does not, the hypothesis fails to explain the formation of all the variables in question, and is said to be *incomplete*. As to the choice of a particular method of solution--e.g., of the way in which the relations are grouped into sub-sets--it is merely a matter of convenience.

SUPPLEMENTARY LECTURE III

(See also Lectures 19-20.)

We obtain quite a different result if labor market is not as described by the relations (II.1)-(II.4) but, instead, by the following relations (the "classical" description of the labor market):

$$\text{(III.1)}\quad n^s = \sigma(W/P)$$

$$\text{(III.2)}\quad n^d = \delta(W/P)$$

$$\text{(III.3)}\quad n = n^s$$

$$\text{(III.4)}\quad n = n^d$$

$$\text{(III.5)}\quad P = \overline{P}$$

Note that we have taken over the "price-control" assumption (II.5). We might replace it by (II.5'), (II.6), (II.7), ("quantity theory of money"), as a rather crude and unrealistic possibility. For a more complete discussion of the "demand sub-set" of the set of relations intended to describe the economic system, see p. II.77, last paragraph.

The new ("classical") set-up can be said to differ from that of Lecture II in two respects:

(a) Workers as well as employers are now assumed to respond to *real wage rates* only. A proportionate change of W and P does not affect either the demand or the supply of labor. People have *"no money illusion"*. This assumption is stated in (III.1), (III.2).

(b) *Demand for labor equals its supply*, $n^d = n^s$. As before, the absence of slavery and the inability of workers to "force themselves" into jobs can be described by the "institutional equation " (II.3); employment equals supply or demand, whichever is smaller. But since demand equals supply, employment equals both. We thus have (III.3), (III.4).

The equality of demand and supply in a market is often called an "equilibrium condition", and is but an abbreviation of the following (dynamic) proposition: whenever demand differs from supply, a quick change in the price of the good or service in question (labor in our case) annihilates this difference. Thus demand does not always equal supply; but the price change necessary to make them equal is so quick that we can neglect the period during which there is appreciable difference between demand and supply. We have discussed this already when we met with equilibrium conditions in other markets (commodities, cash).

The system (III.1)-(III.5) can be interpreted as follows: Unions are abolished. Given the price level, the bargaining between individual workers and employers always leads to a quick adjustment of money wage rates, so that, at the resulting real wage rate, supply of labor equals its demand. Alternatively, one can admit the existence of unions but assume that they cannot fix the money wage rate arbitrarily; rather, they seek (and quickly find) the level of money wage rate that (at given prices) equalizes demand and supply of labor.

What are the implications of (III.1)-(III.5) for the ultimate question (raised in Lecture I) of the effect of policy tools upon policy targets? In Lecture II, we pointed to two targets--absence of involuntary unemployment (and of labor shortage), and maximization of employment; and to two tools: fixation of W and fixation of P (the latter fixation possibly replaced by fixation of M). In our present set-up, there cannot be either involuntary unemployment or labor shortage (except for negligibly brief adjustment periods); and no agency can arbitrarily fix the money wage rates. But there remains the question whether the other, still available tool, fixation of P (or of M) can be used to achieve the other desirable aim--viz., to maximize employment.

The answer is: no. For, (III.1)-(III.4) result--as shown on Chart III:1--in a unique pair of values for n and for W/P:

n depends on δ, σ only;
W/P depends on δ, σ only.

CHART III:1

"CLASSICAL" LABOR MARKET: (III.1)-(III.4)

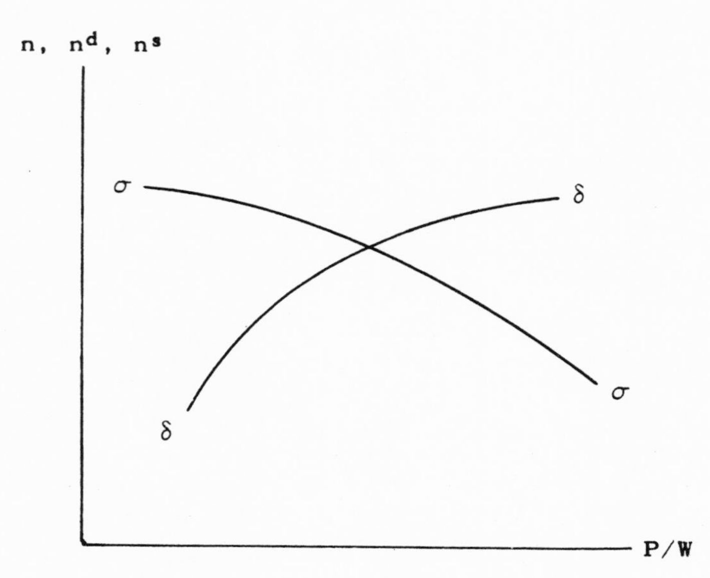

Thus employment n cannot be affected except by changes in the psychological or technological, i.e., in non-controlled, conditions: e.g., less "lazy" workers, better machines. These, and no other conditions also determine the real wage rate. Hence a deliberate change in the price level P will not change either n or W/P; it will merely change W (in the same proportion as P). The inability of raising employment, and hence national real output, y, by price control is illustrated on Chart III:2 which has to be compared with the "non-classical" Chart II:2 after replacing in the latter, the n-scale by a y-scale, where $y = \pi(n)$. The inability of raising employment by control of money stock is illustrated on Chart III:3, which has to be compared with the "non-classical" Chart II:4. In the "non-classical" cases, price or money control could affect real output, at least until a certain output level was reached.

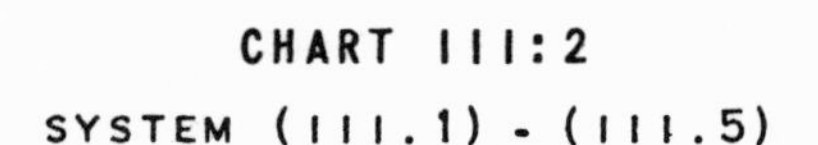

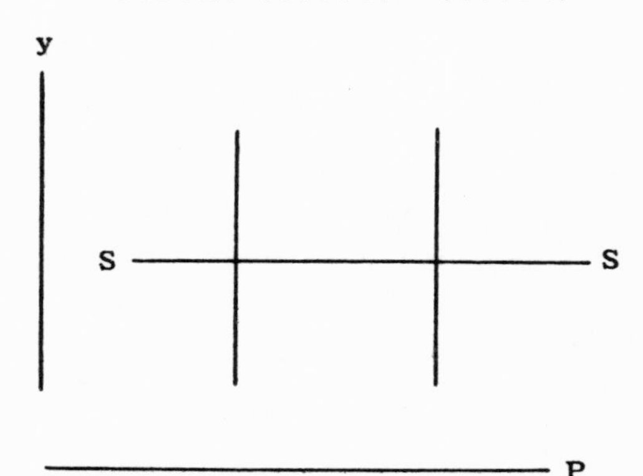

CHART III:3

SYSTEM (III.1)-(III.4), (II.5'), (II.6), (II.7)

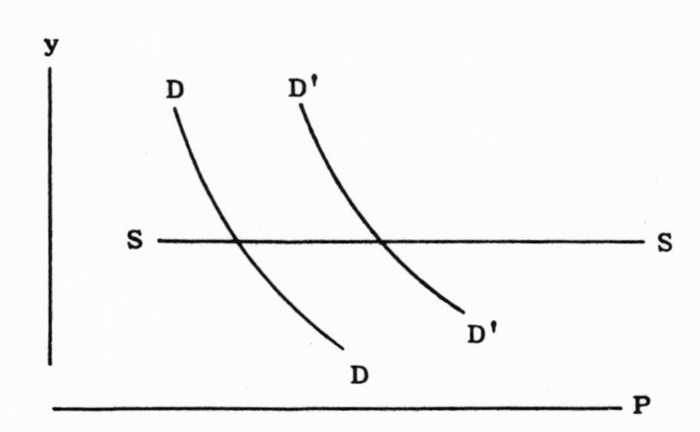

Suppose now that not both classical assumptions (a) and (b) are made but only one of them, while the rest of the system remains as in Lecture II. It can be then shown that price or money control can affect employment.

Thus, combine (III.3), (III.4) (called "assumption of a flexible labor market") with the assumption of money illusion, as in (II.1), (II.2). Graph 19:I shows that in this case employment ($n = n^d = n^s$) is an increasing function of price. Hence by raising price (or money stock) n can be raised. Or, use Chart II:3 where price was fixed at P = 1; and note that as price rises to P = 2, P = 3, ..., the $\delta\delta$-curve shifts upward. The intersection points indicate the values of n and of W determined at given price levels, when $n^d = n^s = n$; and we see that both n and W rise as P (indicated by numbers) rises: Chart III:4.

CHART III:4

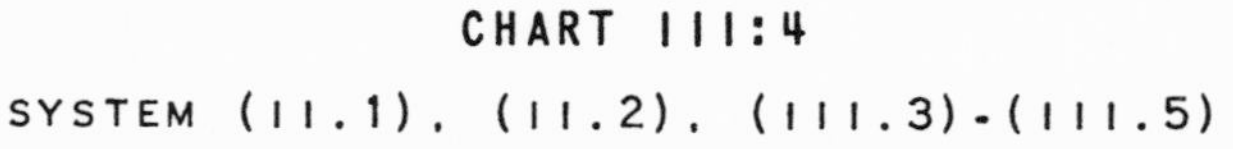

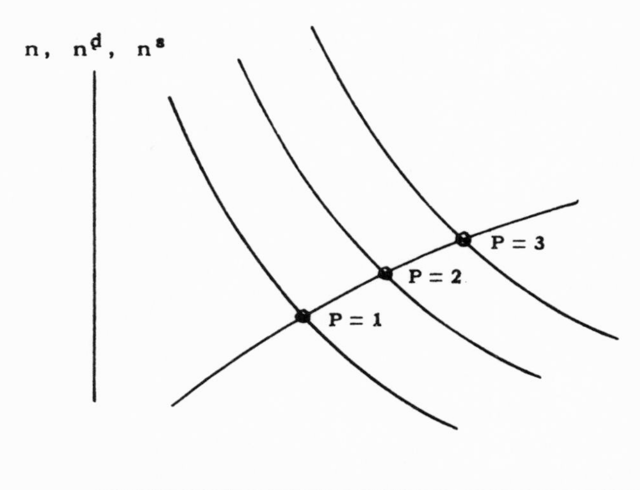

Or, verbally: let P rise. Then the condition $n^s = n^d = n$ makes it impossible for n either to remain constant or to fall. For if n remains constant, then W must have remained constant, since $n = n^s = \sigma(W)$; but, then, in response to risen P at unchanged W, the demand $\delta(W,P) = n^d = n$ must have risen: a contradiction. On the other hand, if n falls, then W must have fallen since $n = n^s = \sigma(W)$ and since σ is an increasing function of W; but, at the same time, because of fallen W and risen P, $\delta(W,P) = n^d = n$ must have risen: again a contradiction. Hence n cannot remain constant or fall when P rises. Hence n rises. --Finally, as an illustration of the analytic method of proof, very useful in the discussion of economic policies, assume σ and δ linear:

$$\text{(III.A)} \quad n = \sigma_o + \sigma_W W = \delta_o + \delta_W W + \delta_P P,$$

where σ_o, σ_W, δ_o, δ_W, δ_P are constants describing, respectively, the (linear) demand and supply functions. *Let* the rise of P by one unit result in the rise of n and W by, respectively, n' and W' units, and see whether these increments are positive or negative. We have

$$\text{(III.B)} \quad n + n' = \sigma_o + \sigma_W(W + W') = \delta_o + \delta_W(W + W') + \delta_p(P + 1).$$

Subtract (III.A) from (III.B):

$$\text{(III.C)} \quad n' = \sigma_W W' = \delta_W W' + \delta_P,$$

and first solve for the unknown increment W':

$$W' = \delta_P/(\sigma_W - \delta_W);$$

We see that W' is positive because, by Propositions 1 and 2 (Lecture II),

$$\sigma_W > 0, \ \delta_W < 0, \ \delta_P > 0.$$

And since by (III.C) $n' = \sigma_W W'$, n' is also positive. That is, n and W change on the same direction as P. This is the gist of the analytic method for this kind of problem ("implicit differentiation of a system of equations with respect to a parameter"-- in our case, this parameter was the "policy tool" P): calculus "in th small" does, in effect, assume linearity, though only for small changes of variables. (See also p. 19.58 and problem 81.)

We have shown that combining the classical "flexible labor market" (III.3), (III.4) with money illusion (II.1), (II.2) leads to a non-classical result. Similarly, the combining of "unionized market" (II.3), (II.4) with the classical absence of money illusion, leads to a non-classical result. On Chart III:1 replace the scale of P/W by a scale of P; then for W = 1 the graph remains the same; the broken line consisting of the lower segments of the two intersecting curves gives the relation between employment n and P when W = 1. For W fixed at a different level, the broken line shifts. We see that, for a given W, employment n depends on P--it first rises, then falls in response to rising P. Hence physical output can be affected by fixing P (or M).

To sum up: The two classical assumptions--"absence of money illusion" and "flexible labor market", *if combined*, yield the classica result--viz., make physical output completely determined by psycho logical and technological conditions, independent of price fixatio or monetary policy.

PROBLEMS

PROBLEM 11. A certain community consists of an *equal* number of "rich" and "poor" families. In a certain ("basic") year the income of each rich family, measured in appropriate money units, was $1 + k$, the income of each poor family was $1 - k$. Therefore the average income was 1. k ("average deviation from average income") can be used in this case as a measure of "income-inequality". Investigations of consumers' habits, carried out in the past (or in different communities) have revealed that if a family has income X, its consumption expenditure is

$$(11.\text{I}) \quad B = q + rX - sX^2 \equiv \beta(X)$$

where q, r, s are all non-negative. Suppose now that while average income remains 1, the income-inequality k changes. Denoting the average consumption expenditure by C show how C depends on k. Plot this relation for k ranging from 0 to 1 assuming

(1) $q = 0$, $r = 0.8$, $s = 0.1$, and

(2) $q = 0$, $r = 0.8$, $s = 0.0$.

Discuss the economic meaning of the cases $k = 0$, $k = 1$, and $s = 0$.

PROBLEM 12. The "individual consumption function" β is the same as in Problem 11, viz., (11.I). The situation in the basic year is also the same. But suppose now the income of each rich as well as of each poor family changes by $(Y - 1)$ money units, and therefore becomes, respectively, $Y + k$ and $Y - k$; therefore the average income becomes Y. Derive the "collective consumption function" that will be valid in this case, i.e., show how C will vary with varying Y. Plot this relation, for Y ranging from 0 to 2, assuming again

(1) $q = 0$, $r = 0.8$, $s = 0.1$

(2) $q = 0$, $r = 0.8$, $s = 0.0$,

and giving k, in each case, two alternative values: $k = 0$ and $k = 0.3$. Compare with the diagram of the individual consumption function β given in (11.I). Discuss the economic implications of the case $s = 0$ and the case $k = 0$.

PROBLEM 13. The individual consumption function is the same as in the two previous problems. So is the basic year's average income and income distribution. Suppose now the income of each family is changed in proportion $Y : 1$. Then the average income becomes Y, the income of each rich family becomes $(1 + k)Y$, and the income of each poor family becomes $(1 - k)Y$. Derive the collective consumption function, and draw diagrams analogous to those of Problem 12.

PROBLEM 14. Show that in both Problems 12 and 13, the collective consumption per family is smaller than the individual consumption β. Extend the discussion to the case of more than two income classes--e.g., to the case of 40 million classes, each consisting of one family.

PROBLEM 15. Write n^s = supply of labor (in mill. man-years)
n^d = demand for labor (in mill. man-years)
n = employment (in mill. man-years)
p = price level (relative to that of 1948)
W = wage rate (in $ per man-hour)
y = real income (in bill. dollars at prices of 1948)

Assume the following equations to be valid:

$$n^s = 60$$

$$n^d = 59.5 + (p/W).$$

$$y = 4n.$$

Comment on the economic meaning of these assumptions. Find the level at which W must be fixed in order to maintain the price level of 1948 and at the same time equate the demand and the supply of labor. What will then be the money income?

PROBLEM 16. Same as Problem 15, except that it is intended to maintain a price level which is 1/3 below that of 1948.

PROBLEMS 17 AND 18. Same as, respectively, Problems 15 and 16, except that the demand function for labor is

$$n^d = 64 - W - (2/p).$$

Compare the results with those of Problems 15 and 16.

PROBLEM 19. Let $n^s = 58 + W$
$n^d = 64 - W - (2/p)$
$y = 4n;$

assuming that $n^s = n^d = n$, derive a relation between 1) y and p; 2) W and p; 3) W and y. If p is fixed at $p = 0.5$, what level will be reached by n, y, and W? If W is fixed at $2.00 an hour, what level will be reached by n, y, and p?

PROBLEM 20. Make the same assumptions as in Problem 19 about the production function and labor market. In addition, assume that 1) real consumption c is related to real income (*not* to disposable real income) as follows:

$$c = 10 + (3/4)y;$$

that 2) the real demands for investment and government goods (c and g, measured in 1948 dollars) are fixed at, respectively, 20 and 30; and that 3) demand and supply for all goods are equalized. What variables will be affected, and by how much, if real government demand falls from 30 to 29? Illustrate by diagram.

PROBLEM 21. Same as Problem 20, but c, y, i, g are replaced (except in the production function) by C = (pc), Y (= py), I (= pi), G (= pg), and it is assumed that investment and government demands are fixed in monetary units (billion dollars), not in physical units.

PROBLEM 22. Assume the labor market and the production function as in Problem 15, and assume the commodity market as in Problem 21. What variables will be affected, and by how much, if G falls from 30 to 29?

PROBLEM 23. Same as Problem 22, but the labor supply function is

$$n^s = 58 + W/p.$$

PROBLEMS 24-26. The government collects a head tax T (billion dollars) = pt. Modify the models of Problems 20, 21, 23 by assuming that c (or C) depends not on income (y or Y) but on disposable income (y − t or Y − T); investigate the effect of a unit change of t or T.

PROBLEMS 27-29. The government collects a proportional income tax, τY billion dollars. Modify the models of Problems 20, 21, 23 by assuming that the government controls the tax rate τ only; investigate the effect of a change of τ from 0.2 to 0.1, investment being constant.

PROBLEMS 30-32. In Problems 27-29, assume that investment (i or I, depending on the problem) changes by one unit, and investigate the effect of such a change 1) when $\tau = 0.2$; 2) when $\tau = 0.3$. Comment on the "stabilizing" (or "destabilizing"?) effect of high income taxes.

PROBLEM 33. Using some or all of the models given in the previous problems, discuss the effect of a change in consumers' tastes on each of the variables that is permitted to change.

PROBLEM 34. Suppose the tastes of consumers and the number of families are constant; the distribution of incomes and its permissible change are as described in Problem 11. Reformulate some or all of the problems 20-33 accordingly, and give the solutions.

PROBLEM 35. Same as Problem 34, but the total income is not constant; its changes, due to changes in individual incomes, are as described in Problems 12 or 13.

PROBLEM 36. Go over the problems 20-35 and state how the answers (and possibly the problems themselves!) have to be modified if the labor market is described as follows:

$n^s = 58 + W/p$

$n^d = 64 - 2W/p.$

$n = n^s = n^d.$

PROBLEM 37. Assume labor market as in Problem 36, and

$y = 4n$

$c = 10 + (3/4)y$

$y^d = c + (I + G)/p$

$y^d = y.$

Indicate the effect of a change in I + G from 50 to 49.

PROBLEM 38. Modify Problem 37 by assuming labor supply to be

$n^s = 58 + W.$

PROBLEM 39. Modify Problem 38 by assuming

$n = \min (n^d, n^s).$

PROBLEMS 40-42. Use the models of Problems 3, 20, and 27, to show what may cause a rise in consumption.

PROBLEM 43. The consumption function is $C = (1/2)\ Y + 10$; investment (defined as annual private demand for investment goods *plus* annual government demand) = 70. What is the difference between investment and saving when (1) income = 150; (2) income = 170; (3) income = 160.

PROBLEM 44. Using the same definition of investment as in the preceding problem, solve the following paradox: 1) If consumption rises, total demand and therefore total income rises; 2) If consumption rises, saving falls; therefore, by the "multiplier principle" total income falls. (HINT: Remember the Problems 40-42).

PROBLEM 45. In Problem 43, assume income at a year's end to be 160 a year, and assume the following behavior on the part of producers: supply equals the demand of preceding month. Let the annual rate of government demand increase on January 1 by 16 and construct the following table:

	DEC. 31	JAN. 1	FEB. 1	MAR. 1	APR. 1	MAY 1	INFINITY
(1) Total Demand							
(2) Total Supply							
(3) Total Income							
(4) Demand *minus* Supply							
(5) Investment *minus* Saving							

Represent these time series on a diagram. On the same diagram plot the corresponding time series for the case when the supply lags behind demand not by a month but by a week.

PROBLEM 46. Same as Problem 45, but the "multiplier" is 4.

PROBLEM 47. Same as Problem 45, but there is a month's lag not only in the response of the producers to changing demand, but also in the response of consumers to changing income.

PROBLEM 48. The consumption function is

$$C = (Y - T)/2 + 10,$$

where T = tax revenue.

Private investment I = 40; the government budget is balanced at G = T = 30; and the total supply and total demand are balanced. The government raises its expenditure by 16, but keeps the budget balanced. Assuming a month's lag on the part of producers compute the relevant time series, as in Problem 45. Compare the results with your answer to Problem 3.

PROBLEM 49. Same as Problem 48, but the government has initially a deficit of 10 and an expenditure of 20; then raises its expenditure by 16, financing this expenditure entirely by taxes.

PROBLEM 50. Formulate algebraically the following assumption: the monthly rate of change of supply is proportional to the difference between demand and supply. How is this assumption related to the corresponding assumption of Problem 45?

PROBLEM 51. Formulate algebraically the following assumption: the rate of increase of money-wage rate, measured in $ per hour per year, equals one-third the difference between labor demand and labor supply, measured in million man-years. Assuming the same demand and supply functions in the labor market as in Problem 19, and assuming a constant price level p = 1, compute the time series for labor demand, labor supply, and money wage rate, starting with an initial money wage rate $W_o = 3$.

PROBLEM 52. In the previous Problem, the "flexibility" of money wage rate can be said to equal 1/3. In what units is flexibility measured?

PROBLEMS 53-54. Same as Problem 51, but flexibility equals, respectively, 1/10 and 5/4.

PROBLEM 55. Discuss the analogies and differences between the description of the market for the "output as a whole" in Problem 50, and the description of the market for labor in Problem 51.

PROBLEM 56. Suppose that (because of the fear of government competition) each dollar added to government spending diminishes private investment by 100β cents. How is national income affected when government increases its expenditure by one billion dollars, with tax receipts left unchanged (assume the marginal propensity to consume = 3/4; and β = either 0.5 or 0.2).

PROBLEM 57. Same as Problem 56, except that all government spendin is financed by taxes. Consumption is a linear function of disposable income.

PROBLEM 58. Modify Problem 57 by assuming that one part of the tax hits the entrepreneurs and thus discourages investment; so that for every dollar increase of tax receipts, investment falls by a dime. (This is in addition to the fall in investment due to the fear of government competition).

PROBLEM 59. Suppose investment demand depends on government expenditure and on taxes, thus: $I = \beta_o - \beta_G G - \beta_T T$. What meaning can be attached to the expression "autonomous change of investment," and "investment multiplier of income?"

PROBLEM 60. Suppose investment consists of two parts: one part ("autonomous") is independent of national income; the other part ("induced" by expectation of future receipts) is equal to 1/6 of disposable national income. How does an increase of autonomous investment by $1 billion affect national income if the marginal propensity to consume is 1/2? Generalize by substituting, respectively, β_1 and α_1 for 1/6 and 1/2.

PROBLEM 61. Under conditions of Problem 60 determine the effect upon national income of a) an increase of government spending, with tax receipts unchanged; b) an increase of tax-receipts, with government spending unchanged; c) an equal increase of tax-receipts and government spending.

PROBLEM 62. Suppose interest rate is controlled by the government. Suppose consumers' saving does not depend on interest rate; but the entrepreneurs demand the more investment goods the lower the interest rate: the latter's fall by 1 per cent (e.g., from 5 to 4 or from 4 to 3 per cent) raises investment by 4 billion dollars. If the marginal propensity to consume is 3/4, how is income affected by a fall of the interest rate from 3 to 2 1/2%?

PROBLEM 63. Suppose that both consumption and investment depend on disposable income as well as on interest rate, so that the private demand for goods rises by $0.9 billion when disposable annual income rises by $1 billion; and falls by 3 billion if interest rate rises by 1%. The government controls the interest rate as well as its own receipts and expenditures. Determine the change in interest rate that is necessary to offset the effect of a given change in the government expenditure upon national income, assuming tax receipts constant.

PROBLEM 64. Same as Problem 63, but instead of keeping tax receipts constant the government maintains a balanced budget.

PROBLEM 65. The government controls not the interest rate but the supply of money. The demand for money consists of two parts: the one is proportional to national income, the other depends linearly on interest rate. Specifically, the first part equals three months' income; the second part rises by $5 billion if interest rate falls by 1%. The demand for goods is as described in Problem 63. The demands for money and for goods balance the respective supplies. Determine the change in income caused by the addition of $10 billion to the money supply.

PROBLEM 66. Represent graphically the conditions of Problem 65. Plot the demand function for money stock $m = (y/4) + \lambda(r)$, using the interest rate r as the horizontal and the money stock m as the vertical axis: the demand function for money will be represented by a family of lines, each line corresponding to a fixed value of the income y. The conditions in the market for goods (supply = demand) will help to pick out the level of interest-rate corresponding to each y. Thus a correspondence between y and m is established.

PROBLEM 67. As in Problem 65, the demand function for money stock as well as the demand function for the output as a whole are linear. Make a change in the numerical conditions so as to make equilibrium income almost proportionate to money stock independently of interest rate (i.e., to make the old "equation of exchange" valid).

PROBLEM 68. Make a change in the numerical conditions of Problem 66 (while maintaining all functions linear) so as to make equilibrium income almost independent of money stock.

PROBLEM 69. Consider Graph 16:I (in course Notes, Lecture 16). Complete the lower diagram, (B), for M = 90, M = 100, ... under the assumption that the interest rate becomes less and less sensitive to changes in money supply as the money supply reaches higher and higher levels. What conclusion follows as to the effect of money supply upon the national income: (1) when money supply is small, and (2) when it is very large?

PROBLEM 70. The conditions in the labor market, and the production function are as in Problem 19. The government fixes *dollar* values of government expenditure (G) and of money supply (M). There is no "money illusion" on the part of private persons. Thus:

$$c = 10 + (3/4)\ y$$

$$i = (1/20)\ y - 3r$$

$$y = c + i + (G/p);$$

the demand for money stock (*real* value) is

$$m^d = (y/4) - 15\ r;$$

and

$$pm^d = M^s.$$

From the last 5 equations compute a relation between y and p, the "demand function for the output as a whole", the quantities G and M^s being given. Confront this result with the relation between y and p derived from the labor market and production conditions, by plotting both relations in the (y,p)-plane, for one or two fixed values of G and M. Find the equilibrium values of y and p, for 1) G = 0, M = 80; 2) G = 0, M = 100; 3) G = 10, M = 80; 4) G = 10, M = 100.

PROBLEM 71. Same as Problem 70, but M cannot be fixed independently of G because government spending is financed entirely by borrowing from banks (or by printing money). Suppose that at the beginning, G = 0, M = 80; then increase G to 10 (10 billion dollars a year) and calculate the equilibrium values of y and p after 6 months 1 year, 2 years.

PROBLEM 72. Same as Problem 71, with the following two modifications (to be taken together): 1) government spending is financed as follows: 25% by borrowing from banks, 25% by borrowing from the public, and 50% by taxes; 2) in the consumption function and the investment function (given in Problem 70) replace real income y by real disposable income y', defined as follows:

$$y' = y - (T + B)/p,$$

where T = annual tax receipts, and B = the dollar amount borrowed from the public annually. (No servicing of the government debt has begun during the period considered.)

PROBLEM 73. Same as Problem 72 but the government's annual repayment (with interest) of its debt to the public and to the banks equals respectively 20% and 40% of the sums currently borrowed from them.

PROBLEM 74. Of the four cases stated at the end of Problem 70, consider the first case only, i.e., fix G = 0, M = 80. Find the equilibrium values for y and p. Now assume that the behavior of workers has changed: the supply function has shifted from

$$n^s = 58 + W$$

to

$$n^s = 58 + (3/4)\ W,$$

(i.e., the same amount of labor is offered at a money wage rate reduced by 25%). How does this shift affect the price level, the real income, and the employment?

PROBLEM 75. Suppose the interest rate is known to be 2 per cent, a level at which it does not respond to changes in money supply, so that the liquidity preference equation of Problem 70 (and 74) becomes $m^d = (y/4) = 30$. Solve Problems 70 and 74 under this modification (unless you find them overdetermined).

PROBLEMS 76-77. Make simultaneously the following changes in Problem 70: 1) the demand for both consumer's and investment goods responds to changes, not only in real income and in interest rate, but also in the real value of the money stock. Let us say,

$$c + i = 0.8y - 3r + 2m;$$

2) the interest rate is constant, $r = 2$. Solve Problems 70 and 74 (unless you find them overdetermined).

PROBLEM 78. Modify Problem 70 by assuming the following conditions in the labor market: the labor demand and labor supply function (and the production function) as in Problem 19; but labor supply and labor demand are not equalized. Instead,

$$n = \min (n^s, n^d).$$

(HINT: Use a diagram to avoid pitfalls.)

PROBLEMS 79-80. Use the conditions of Problem 78 to answer the same questions as in Problems 74 and 75, respectively, assuming, instead of a shift in the workers' supply function, a change in the money wage rate fixed by collective bargaining agencies.

PROBLEM 81. Assume that (1) demand for labor and supply of labor cannot be different for a period longer than one month; (2) the demand for labor depends on the real wage rate only; (3) the supply of labor is (numerically) more elastic with respect to money wage rate than with respect to price level; i.e., an increase in money wage rate in a given proportion, at constant price level, elicits a larger increase in the labor supply than a decrease in price level in the same proportion, at a constant wage rate level.

Give a graphical proof and a verbal proof that, under these assumptions, an increase in the price level is followed, after at most one month, by an *increase* in employment.

ADVICE. An easy graphical proof can be provided by plotting real wage rates against demand and supply. For the verbal proof, show that, under the given assumptions, price increase cannot result in either falling or unchanged employment.

COURSE EXAMINATION
Fall 1949

Duration: 2 hours

REMARKS.

A. The following problems deal with two properties attributed to unemployment relief: 1) it reduces the incentive to work, therefore diminishes employment; 2) it increases consumption, therefore increases employment. You will be required to bring clarity in this matter, using few words.

B. The word "real" means "measured in dollars of constant purchasing power." In some propositions, this adjective, or its opposite ("money") can be omitted without ambiguity.

C. The word "relief" means "unemployment relief." Relief rate and wage rate are measured in dollars per hour or week.

PROBLEM I. ASSUMPTIONS.

1. Demand for labor depends on real wage rate only.

2. Supply of labor depends on the excess of real wage rate over real relief rate only.

3. Demand for labor equals its supply and equals employment.

4. The government fixes the real relief rate.

Comment on policy implications of these assumptions taken jointly.

PROBLEM II. ASSUMPTIONS AND DEFINITIONS.

5. The government fixes a proportional tax rate on income.

6. The government fixes its real demand for goods.

7. The businessmen fix real investment.

8. Demand for goods consists of real consumption, real government demand, and real investment.

9. Demand for goods equals real income.

10. Real consumption depends on real disposable income only.

11. Disposable income equals income minus taxes plus relief.

12. Unemployment is the excess of labor force over employment.

13. Real income equals employment times productivity (of labor).

14. Labor force and productivity are determined by variables other than those listed here or in Problem I.

Considering Assumptions 5-14 together with the Assumption 4 of Problem I, show that certain government controlled variables determine unemployment.

Show that Assumptions 1-14 are inconsistent.

PROBLEM III.

Accept Assumptions 1-4 after replacing Assumptions 1 and 2 by the following more specific ones (labor measured in million-men, wage and relief rates in dollars per hour):

1a. Demand for labor equals 61 minus real wage rate.

2a. Supply of labor equals 59 plus real wage rate minus relief rate.

How does an increase in relief rate affect employment?

PROBLEM IV.

Accept Assumptions 4-14 after replacing Assumptions 5 and 10 by the following more specific ones:

5a. Tax equals 1/6 of income.

10a. Real consumption equals a constant plus 5/6 of real disposable income.

Show that, if labor productivity per man-week rises by $1 (of constant purchasing power), and if the real relief rate is the only other exogenous variable permitted to change, then, in order to keep unemployment below 4% of the labor force, the real relief rate per man-week must increase by more than $8.80. Comment on the size of this figure.

PROBLEM V.

Comment on the contradiction between the results of III and IV. Then replace, in the Assumptions 2a and 4, real wage and relief rates by money wage and relief rates, while retaining all other Assumptions of Problems III and IV. Will this remove the contradiction? Give an economic (non-numerical) comment on the changes that the money relief rate has to undergo to counteract "technological unemployment." How will this result change if other government measures (which?) are permitted, or if investment is not autonomous?

SOME SUGGESTIONS FOR READING

Books:

Keynes, John M. — *The General Theory of Employment, Interest and Money*, New York: Harcourt Brace and Co., 1936, 403 pp.

Harris, Seymour E. (ed.) — *The New Economics.* Keynes' Influence on Theory and Public Policy, New York: Alfred A. Knopf, Inc., 1947, 686 pp.

Klein, Lawrence R. — *The Keynesian Revolution*, New York: Macmillan Co., 1947, 218 pp.

Lange, Oscar — *Price Flexibility and Employment*, Cowles Commission Monograph No. 8, Bloomington, Indiana: The Principia Press, 1944, 114 pp.

Lerner, A.P., and F.D. Graham (ed.) — *Planning and Paying for Full Employment*, Princeton: Princeton University Press, 1946, 222 pp.

Terborgh, George — *The Bogey of Economic Maturity*, Chicago: Machinery and Allied Products Institute, 1945, 263 pp.

Wright, David M. — *The Economics of Disturbance*, New York: Macmillan and Co., 1947, 114 pp.

De Chazeau, M., et al. (Committee for Economic Development Research Study) — *Jobs and Markets: How to Prevent Inflation and Depression*, New York and London: McGraw-Hill Book Co., Inc., 1946, 143 pp.

Hansen, Alvin H. — *Economic Policy and Full Employment*, New York: McGraw-Hill Book Co., Inc., 1947, 340 pp.

Metzler, L., E. Domar, et al. — *Income, Employment and Public Policy, Essays in Honor of Alvin H. Hansen*, New York: W.W. Norton and Co., Inc., 1948, 379 pp.

Klein, Lawrence R. — *Economic Fluctuations in the United States, 1921-1941*, Cowles Commission Monograph No. 11, New York: John Wiley and Sons, Inc., 1950, 174 pp.

Articles:

Hicks, John R. — "Mr. Keynes and the Classics: A Suggested Interpretation," *Econometrica*, Vol. 5, April, 1937, pp. 147-159.

Mints, L.W., A.H. Hansen, et al. — "A Symposium on Fiscal and Monetary Policy," *Review of Economic Statistics*, Vol. 28, May, 1946, pp. 60-84.

Modigliani, Franco — "Liquidity Preference and the Theory of Interest and Money," *Econometrica*, Vol. 12, January, 1944, pp. 45-88.

Mosak, J. and A. Smithies — "Forecasting Post-War Demand: Discussion," *Econometrica*, Vol. 13, January, 1945, pp. 54-59.